CONTRACANTO A WALT WHITMAN

———————

COUNTERSONG TO WALT WHITMAN

AND OTHER POEMS

Pedro Mir
Photograph: Joseph Shneberg

PEDRO MIR

CONTRACANTO A WALT WHITMAN

———————————

COUNTERSONG TO WALT WHITMAN

AND OTHER POEMS

TRANSLATED BY

JONATHAN COHEN AND DONALD D. WALSH

PEEPAL TREE

Published in Great Britain in 2017
Peepal Tree Press Ltd
17 King's Avenue
Leeds LS6 1QS
UK

First published in 1993 in this bi-lingual edition
by Azul Editions
who acknowledged the New York Council on the Arts,
which provided support for the translation

© estate of Pedro Mir 1993, 2017
Translation copyright © 1993 Jonathan Cohen
& Mrs. Donald D. Walsh
Introductions © Jean Franco and Silvio Torres-Saillant

Some of these renderings first appeared
in *American Poetry Review, Review,
Street Magazine.*

ISBN 13: 9781845233563

All rights reserved
No part of this publication may be
reproduced or transmitted in any form
without permission

Supported using public funding by
ARTS COUNCIL
ENGLAND

CONTENTS

A POET OF HIS PEOPLE, A POET OF THE WORLD

SILVIO TORRES-SAILLANT

True literary artists bear witness to the challenge of the human condition as it is lived in their particular time and place within the confines of discrete circumstances. The clearer their success in capturing the drama of existence and communicating it to their home public with conviction, the greater their chance of producing texts that speak persuasively to people elsewhere. In the Dominican Republic no one lays a more legitimate claim to intimacy with the yearnings of the Dominican people as well as with the texture of their collective voice than Pedro Mir. No author writing in the country enjoys more popularity and reverence than he among both literary and non-literary readers in virtually all sectors of society.

The agreement by the full multipartisan legislature of the Dominican Congress in 1982 to confer upon Mir the title of National Poet suggests the high regard in which his native audience holds him. In New York, the home of many Dominicans, he was awarded an honorary doctorate from Hunter College in June of 1991 and eight months later he became the subject of a major conference at Hostos Community College. In January 1993 Mir received the National Prize for Literature, the highest honour a literary artist can aspire to in the Dominican Republic. The multitude of voices that celebrated the prize includes spokespersons as distinguished as poet and playwright Manuel Rueda, who dedicated a whole issue of his weekly *Isla Abierta* to Mir. The sentiment of the general public was perhaps best captured by the daily *El Siglo,* whose editorial for the occasion described Mir's best known poem as "the common property of all Dominicans."

7

Born on June 3, 1913, in the southerly city of San Pedro de Macorís, of a Puerto Rican mother and a Cuban father, Mir published his first poems in 1937 through the agency of Juan Bosch, who had already achieved notoriety in Dominican letters. Mir soon attained recognition not only among young intellectuals, who hailed him as a "social poet," but also among the cultural commissars of the Trujillo dictatorship, who viewed him with suspicion. By 1947 it had become clear that he should leave the country. Once he did, the scribes of the regime undertook to suppress his name, as is evident in a Dominican poetry anthology whose first edition in 1943 had prominently displayed his poems but omitted him completely in the second edition of 1951.

Treading the path of exile came without glamour for Mir. Abroad, he did not enjoy the visibility of prestigious political expatriates such as Bosch, who befriended Pedro Henríquez Ureña, Nicolás Guillén, Romulo Gallegos, and Miguel Otero Silva, among other major literary figures of Latin America. Mir did not form part of famous intellectual circles. Rather, he quietly earned a humble living, doing menial jobs, as be continued to write. While in Cuba, in 1949 he published *Hay un país en el mundo* and in 1952 committed to print his *Contracanto a Walt Whitman* during a brief sojourn in Guatemala, where his small collection *Seis momentos de esperanza* also appeared the following year. These publications elicited no fanfare, but they laid the groundwork for the poetics that would thenceforward characterize Mir's *oeuvre.* The epic breadth of his song, the historical incisiveness of his themes, the upliftment of hope as an inexorable dogma, and the lyrical fabric of his verse, all emerge palpably in these thin volumes.

Mir may be said to have consistently worshipped the muse of history, and in that faith he shows a striking kinship with typical Caribbean poets of the stature of Aimé Césaire, Nicolás Guillén, and Kamau Brathwaite. In characteristic Antillean fashion, he has also gone outside the realm of verse production to explore historical processes of his country and the larger Caribbean region. His essay *Tres leyendas de colores,* which he completed in 1949 and did not publish until 20 years later, traces the origins of the modern

Caribbean to "the first three revolutions" of the Americas, which took place on the island of Hispaniola. Subsequently, *El gran incendio* (1969), *La raíces dominicanas de la doctrina de Monroe* (1974), the three-volume text *La noción de período en la historia dominicana* (1981-83), and *Historia del hambre* (1987) each combine the prose style of a mature literary craftsman with the rigour of a professional historian to achieve penetrating insights into the most crucial junctures that have shaped the Dominican Republic, its place in world affairs, and the intransigent endurance of its people.

His prose fiction further illustrates Mir's dedication to the historical imagination in the scrutiny of the Caribbean experience. *La gran hazaña de Límber y después otoño* (1977), a collection of three animal fables linked by a cornice, *Cuando amaban las tierras comuneras* (1978), a novel set chronologically between the 1916 and the 1965 military occupations of the Dominican Republic by the United States, and *¡Buen viaje, Pancho Valentín!* (1981), the fictional memoirs of a man returning to the native land after a long absence, derive most of their dramatic tension from the historical imperatives that frame the characters and the dilemmas they encounter.

Mir has produced considerable work in the fields of history, fiction, and even art criticism and theory, in which he has written *Apertura a la estética* (1974), *Fundamentos de teoría y crítica de arte* (1979), and *La estética del soldadito* (1991). His achievements in other literary genres and areas of intellectual endeavour notwithstanding, his verse remains the best known facet of his writings. Probably to Mir's own chagrin, with him the poet has greatly overshadowed the essayist, the fiction writer, and the thinker. But that has to do with the fact that when he came back from his long exile in 1962, following the death of Trujillo, it was as a poet that he first won the hearts of his native audience. His poetry recitals in the 1960s and 1970s attracted large and enthusiastic crowds of workers, students, and cultural activists in Santo Domingo and cities of the interior. The popularity of *Hay un país en el mundo,* which became "the common property of all Dominicans" as soon as the poet regained his homeland, has continued unabated. Not only has the poem gone through innumerable reprintings and frequent staged choral readings, but it has inspired several renditions by artists working in other forms, such as painting, etching, music, and photography.

For many years following his return, Mir's reputation rested largely on the published poems he brought from exile. However, he subsequently produced major poetic texts that supplement and deepen the known elements of his verse. Moved by the deaths of the Mirabal sisters, whose brutal murder by the agents of the tyrant on November 25, 1960, had shaken all layers of Dominican society, Mir produced *Amén de mariposas* (1969), a poem in which he successfully retakes the epic mode to explore the historical roots of the horror. In *Poemas de buen amor y a veces de fantasía* (1969), a sequence of sonnets and other lyric poems, he aims to historicize the realm of Eros by delving into the pleasures of the human body and placing love and sex within materialistically explainable parameters.

The next volume of verse by Mir, entitled *Viaje a la muchedumbre* (1971), consists of thirteen poems, the majority of which are linked thematically by the search for a principle of coherence to harmonize the individual and the collective and to cancel out the presumed dichotomy between self and community. The following year a short selection of his poems published by Siglo XXI Editores in Mexico, under the editorship of Jaime Labastida, borrowed the title *Viaje a la muchedumbre* (1972). Oddly enough, the Siglo XXI anthology neglected to mention that the title had come from an existing volume, nor did it include the sonnet "Viaje a la muchedumbre," the text that gave the original collection its name. As with any selection, the Mexican anthology gives a partial picture of the scope and amplitude of Mir's poetry. But despite its shortcomings, it has played a decisive role in enhancing the international visibility of the poet. Though most readers outside the Dominican shores who have read him have done so through Labastida's selection, there is much more to Mir. Suffice it to mention *El huracán Neruda* (1975), a major epic poem which remains his last known work in verse. Hinging thematically on two onerous Chilean deaths, that of President Salvador Allende and that of the immense Pablo Neruda, which occurred both in September 1973 within twelve days of each other, the poem convincingly moves from threnody to exultation. The dark shadows cast upon the peoples of the Americas by the demise of two bright beacons of hope are refashioned into a source of light. The poem illustrates a dynamic whereby the sense of history gets placed on the rails toward a vision of utopia. In that sense, the text furthers the hopeful worldview that prevails in all of Mir's works throughout his five decades of rich literary production.

Like few other poets of his or any other generation whether at home or abroad, Mir has forged a diction that has placed him incontestably as the foremost epic singer of his people's experience. In that respect, his achievement parallels the glorious feat he himself attributes to Whitman as the supreme interpreter of the American collective at one given point in history. In *Contracanto a Walt Whitman*, a text in which the great poet "of Manhattan the son" serves as vehicle for an epopeia of the relationship between the United States and the rest of the Americas, the speaker rhetorically asks:

> For
> > what has a great undeniable poet been
> > > but a crystal-clear pool
> > > > where a people discover their perfect
> > > > > likeness? ...

> And what
> > but the chord of a boundless guitar
> > > where the fingers of the people play
> > > > their simple, their own, their strong and
> > > > > true innumerable song?
> (Tr. Cohen)

Dominicans have undoubtedly spotted their perfect likeness in the verse of Mir. Whenever people of other nationalities have come upon his poetry, they too have seen themselves in it. The high esteem his work has received from readers in other parts of Latin America and the Caribbean is greater than one could reasonably expect given its limited international diffusion. Were he from a country with official institutions devoted to supporting, preserving, and exporting the nation's most valuable cultural products, his worldwide reputation would equal that of the best known authors today. Even so, his work has travelled. Partial translations of his poems exist at least in Russian, Armenian, French, and English. The present bilingual edition, the amplest collection of his poetry to appear in any language thus far, will give both Spanish- and English-speaking readers in the United States the opportunity to recognize themselves in the poetic visage of one of the most authentic literary artists to have come from the Caribbean. Readers will find here a voice that speaks to the world as urgently as it does to the Dominican people.

FOREWORD TO THE COUNTERSONG

JEAN FRANCO

The *Countersong to Walt Whitman* by the Dominican poet Pedro Mir was first published in Guatemala in 1952, not long before Colonel Castillo Armas overthrew the elected President, Jacobo Arbenz, and initiated that country's long and continuing agony. I was living in Guatemala at that time; it was there that I learned something of what it meant to be born and to live in Central America and the Caribbean. On the long boat-ride from Amsterdam, we had docked in Ciudad Trujillo, the then capital of the Dominican Republic. Fat rats climbed over the corrugated roofs of the scalding wharfs and Trujillo's police would not let us land because we were bound for "red" Guatemala.

In the then flourishing Casa de la Cultura of Guatemala City, I met exiles from all over the continent, from Trujillo's island, from Batista's Cuba, from Somoza's Nicaragua, from Rojas Pinilla's Colombia, from Pérez Jiménez's Venezuela. The grammatical possessive is, in this case, not simply a rhetorical device since these countries were fiefdoms whose dictators were usually maintained in power by U.S. support. Many of the exiles dreamed of an emancipated Latin America as a place where a generous vision of social justice might eventually prevail. What in fact followed was the invasion of Guatemala (1954), of the Dominican Republic (1965), the Brazilian military coup (1964), the destabilization and overthrow of the Allende regime in Chile (1973), not to mention the more recent interventions in Grenada and Panama.

Ever since the Uruguayan critic Enrique Rodó published his *Ariel* in 1900, Latin Americans had tended to view the Mexican-American

13

border as separating two rival versions of civilization. Two of Mir's great contemporaries, Pablo Neruda in his *Canto General* (1950) and Nicolás Guillén in *West Indies Ltd.* (1934), had also addressed themselves defiantly to the United States in order to affirm Latin American difference. The fact that Mir's work is less known than these has much to do with his place of birth, the Dominican Republic — whose literature still today is far less translated and disseminated than that of other Caribbean countries. It also has to do with his long exile from his homeland.

Mir's dialogue with Whitman belongs to a longstanding tradition. Whitman had been an icon to Latin Americans ever since the Cuban poet José Martí heard him speak in 1887, at what would be his last public appearance in New York. Martí's description fixed his image as a poet-prophet far above mere mortals. He wrote, "He [Whitman] seemed like a god last night, seated on a throne of red velvet, with his white hair, his beard falling on his chest, his eyebrows thick as a forest, his hand resting on a cane." Whitman's words, according to Martí, resembled the murmur of planets. But perhaps what most attracted Latin Americans, even those like Nicaragua's Rubén Darío who believed democracy to be at odds with art, was his American idiom and his claim to represent a New World.

Mir's poem is both a celebration of Whitman and an assertion of difference — a celebration of the poet of the common people and a denunciation of the "manifest destiny" of the nation that Whitman has helped to build. Whitman had brought together all the peoples of the United States into one choral and prophetic voice, "orotund, sweeping and final," and now it is the turn of people from outside those borders, the anonymous, marginalized inhabitant of Quisqueya, the Caribbean island which is now divided between the Dominican Republic and Haiti. Thus Mir both follows Whitman and diverges. He follows Whitman across a pristine America and identifies with its founding spirit, even with the Whitmanian *I* which, like a Leibnitzian monad, is "the revolving of all mirrors / around a single image." It is this self-affirmation that has given birth to the United States.

But here the two poets must diverge. Something has come

between pure self-affirmation and fulfilment and that something is money, the simulacrum that replaces reality and which alienates human beings from the self. Mir here comes closest to Ernesto Cardenal's vision of a fallen humanity as he traces the degeneration of the Whitmanian *I* and its resurrection as imperial egoism that has commodified Latin America and deprived the nations of the continent of their autonomy. Whitman's spirit can only be redeemed by a new pronoun, the *we* of all those nations and peoples that have been "othered."

With the possible exception of Cardenal, few poets today would see Latin America's future with such self-confidence. For the times are different and poetry once again seems to be withdrawing from a civic function. Can the translation of such a poem do more than offer us a missing element of Latin America's past? Or can it during this difficult fin de siècle restore a tenuous hope — that the triumph of cynical reason may only be temporary?

TRANSLATION NOTE

JONATHAN COHEN

Readers of verse translations are entitled to an explanation of how translators define the aims of their work, given that the approaches to translating poetry range from very literal to very liberal. I can say a few words on behalf of the late Donald Walsh (1903-80) because I worked closely with him on various translation projects during the last decade of his life. We collaborated on translating poems by Ernesto Cardenal for a collection that Walsh edited for New Directions, as well as poems by Pedro Mir and other Latin American poets for a special issue of *Street Magazine* that I edited. Through our work together, I got to know him as a translator, and to admire him.

A distinguished Spanish teacher for most of his life (for several years the editor of *Hispania,* the journal of the American Association of Teachers of Spanish and Portuguese, and then the director of the foreign language program of the Modern Language Association), he was not motivated to make translations for the main purpose of discovering how they would extend the range and capacity of poetry in English. He was, however, very much committed to advocating for Spanish-language poetry, especially that from Latin America, by translating and editing several books of it — a labour of love to which he devoted himself with remarkable energy during the years of his retirement.

He once told me that the translator should say in English *only* what the poet says, not what the poet might have wanted to say. At the same time, he did not insist on "dictionary" (word-for-word) translations. He preferred translations that would offer readers a fair paraphrase of the poet's words, without any attempt to improve on them.

In an essay on translation, he described what he considered the translator's proper approach:

> The translator's first task is to discover exactly what the author has said, his ideas and the way he has expressed them. He must understand and respond to the tone and the overtones of each of the author's words and phrases. He must try to re-create in his language the miraculous fusion of thought and expression that produced the original work.... The translator's role is humble and secondary but nonetheless crucial: to bring over into his language a work that is worthy of the considerable effort involved in the act of translation. His goal must be to say in the second language what the author said in the first language with as much fidelity as is permitted by the differences in the two languages. And he must do his best to circumvent the obstacles presented by those differences. His duty is to express not himself but his author.[*]

To emphasize his position, he added, "If the careless or ignorant or self-centred translator excuses his vagaries by invoking poetic license, his license ought to be revoked." In theory, my own translation poetics is similar. I do not follow, in a slavish way, the letter of Mir's Spanish. Nor do I assume the liberty not only to vary from the words and sense of the *Countersong to Walt Whitman,* but to forsake them as I see occasion. I translate word for word when precise and poetic enough, and sense for sense when necessary, in an effort to create a lyric paraphrase that attempts to be faithful to both the meaning and the poetic quality of the original poem.

I have thus tried to use language with real feeling that expresses the poet's ideas and that also sings the way he does in the *Countersong.* Whitman's own words, it should be noted, are used here when called for by the Spanish rendering of them.

If Donald Walsh and I have been successful in realizing our aims to re-create Mir's voice in English, we have made accurate poetic translations that serve him well.

---

* "Some Thoughts on Translation," *Review* (Center for Inter-American Relations) 11 (Spring 1974): 20-22.

VIAJE A LA MUCHEDUMBRE

[JOURNEY TO THE MASSES]

Aquel que entre dos flores razaba un legumbre
no comprendía a voces las veces más sencillas.
Disuadido del tiempo libraba una costumbre
contra todo molino de viento en sus rodillas.

Hasta que un día a raíz de cierta pesadumbre
parpadeada en un sobresalto de las mejillas,
llegó al arrojado rojo de la muchedumbre
y se bañó en la agradable esponja de sus orillas.

Vivo y mojado. Arriba, la lengua de los bronces.
Cerca, una estatua antigua nublada desde entonces
fija en perfecta llovizna hacia la juventud.

Pues cuando el vino baja en doncellas de las vides
no hay ventura más fresca para los no me olvides
que un baño en el rojo arrojo de la multitud.

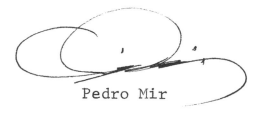

Pedro Mir

HAY UN PAÍS EN EL MUNDO
poema gris en varias ocasiones

¡Ah, desventurados! — exclamó indignado el sirio — ¿Como imaginar semejante exceso de rabia furiosa? Me dan ganas de dar tres pasos y aplastar de tres patadas a todo ese hormiguero de ridículos asesinos ...
   No os toméis ese trabajo — le respondieron —. Ellos mismos se encargan de su ruina.

Voltaire, Micromegas, cap. VII

Hay
un país en el mundo
                colocado
en el mismo trayecto del sol.
Oriundo de la noche.
          Colocado
en un inverosímil archipiélago
de azúcar y de alcohol.
               Sencillamente
liviano,
          como un ala de murciélago
apoyado en la brisa.
               Sencillamente
claro,
               como el rastro del beso en las solteras
antiguas
          o el día en los tejados.
               Sencillamente
frutal. Fluvial. Y material. Y sin embargo

THERE IS A COUNTRY IN THE WORLD

a poem, sad on more than one occasion

"Oh, wretched ones!" cried the Syrian indignantly. "How
can we imagine such an excess of furious rage? I feel like
taking three steps and squashing underfoot that whole
anthill of ridiculous assassins ..."

"Don't go to all that trouble," they answered. "They will
see to their own downfall."

Voltaire, *Micromegas,* VII

There is
a country in the world
                        situated
right in the sun's path.
A native of the night.
                        Situated
in an improbable archipelago
of sugar and alcohol.
                        Simply
light,
        like a bat's wing
leaning on the breeze.
                        Simply
bright,
                        like the trace of a kiss on an elderly
maiden,
        or daylight on the roof tiles.
                        Simply
fruitful. Fluvial. And material. And yet

sencillamente tórrido y pateado
como una adolescente en las caderas.
Sencillamente triste y oprimido.
Sinceramente agreste y despoblado.

En verdad.
Con tres millones
               suma de la vida
y entre tanto
               cuatro cordilleras cardinales
y una inmensa bahía y otra inmensa bahía,
tres penínsulas con isles adyacentes
y un asombro de ríos verticales
y tierra bajo los árboles y tierra
bajo los rios y en la falda del monte
y al pie de la colina y detrás del horizonte
y tierra desde el canto de los gallos
y tierra bajo el galope de los caballos
y tierra sobre el día, bajo el mapa, alrededor
y debajo de todas las huellas y en medio del amor.
Entonces
       es lo que he declarado.
                        Hay
un país en el mundo
sencillamente agreste y despoblado.

simply torrid, abused and kicked
like a young girl's hips.
Simply sad and oppressed.
Sincerely wild and uninhabited.

In truth.
With three million
                    life's sum total
and all the while
                    four cardinal cordilleras
and an immense bay and another immense bay,
three peninsulas with adjacent isles
and the wonder of vertical rivers
and earth beneath the trees and earth
beneath the rivers and at the edge of the forest
and at the foot of the hill and behind the horizon
and earth from the cock's crow
and earth beneath the galloping horses
and earth over the day, under the map, around
and underneath all the footprints and in the midst of love.
Then
        it is as I have said.
                            There is
a country in the world
simply wild and uninhabited.

Algún amor creerá
que en este fluvial país en que la tierra brota,
y se derrama y cruje como una vena rota,
donde el día tiene su triunfo verdadero,
irán los campesinos con asombro y apero
a cultivar
      cantando
           su franja propietaria.

Este amor
quebrará su inocencia solitaria.
                    Pero no.
Y creerá
que en medio de esta tierra recrecida,
donde quiera, donde ruedan montañas por los valles
como frescas monedas azules, donde duerme
un bosque en cada flor y en cada flor la vida,
irán los campesinos por la loma dormida
a gozar
      forcejeando
           con su propia cosecha.
Este amor
doblará su luminosa flecha.
                  Pero no.

Some love will think
that in this fluvial country in which earth blossoms,
and spills over and cracks like a bursting vein,
where day has its true victory,
the farmers will go amazed with their spades
to cultivate
        singing
            their strip of ownership.
This love
will shatter its solitary innocence.
                    But no.

And it will think
that in the midst of this swollen land,
everywhere, where mountains roll through valleys
like fresh blue coins, where a forest
sleeps in each flower and in each flower life,
the farmers will walk along the sleeping ridge
to enjoy
        struggling
            with their own harvest.
This love
will bend its luminous arrow.
                    But no.

Y creerá
de donde el viento asalta el íntimo terrón
y lo convierte en tropas de cumbres y praderas,
donde cada colina parece un corazón,
en cada campesino irán las primaveras
cantando
              entre los surcos
                          su propiedad.
Este amor
alcanzará su floreciente edad.
                          Pero no.

Hay
un país en el mundo
donde un campesino breve,
seco y agrio
              muere y muerde
descalzo
       su polvo derruido,
y la tierra no alcanza para su bronca muerte.
¡Oídlo bien! No alcanza para quedar dormido.
Es un país pequeño y agredido. Sencillamente triste,
triste y torvo, triste y acre. Ya lo dije:
sencillamente triste y oprimido.

And it will think
from where the wind buffets the inmost clod of earth
and transforms it into flocks of peaks and plains,
where each hill seems a heart,
in each farmer spring upon spring will go
singing
      among the furrows
                 his land.
This love
will reach its flowering Age.
               But no.

There is
a country in the world
where a farmer, cut down,
withered and bitter
               dies and bites
barefoot
     his defeated dust,
lacking enough earth for his harsh death.
Listen closely! Lacking earth to go to sleep in.
It is a small and beleaguered country. Simply sad,
sad and grim, sad and bitter. I've already said it,
simply sad and oppressed.

No es eso solamente.
                    Faltan hombres
para tanta tierra. Es decir, faltan hombres
que desnuden la virgen cordillera y la hagan madre
después de unas canciones.
                    Madre de la hortaliza.
Madre del pan. Madre del lienzo y del techo.
Madre solícita y nocturna junto al lecho …
Faltan hombres que arrodillen los árboles y entonces
los alcen contra el sol y la distancia.
Contra las leyes de la gravedad.
Y les saquen reposo, rebeldía y claridad.
Y hombres que se acuesten con la arcilla
y la dejen parida de paredes.
                         Y hombres
que descifren los dioses de los ríos
y los suban temblando entre las redes.
Y hombres en la costa y en los fríos
                              desfiladeros
y en toda desolacíon.
Esto es, faltan hombres.
                    Y falta una canción.

Procedente del fondo de la noche
vengo a hablar de un país.
                    Precisamente
pobre de población.
                    Pero
                    no es eso solamente.

And it's not that alone.
                              Men are needed
for so much land. That is, men are needed
to strip the virgin cordillera and make her a mother
after a few songs.
                              Mother of vegetables.
Mother of bread. Mother of the fence and the roof.
Caring and nocturnal mother at the bedside ...
Men are needed to fell the trees and then
to raise them high against the sun and distance.
Against the laws of gravity.
And to take from them rest, rebellion and light.
And men to lie with the clay
and leave her giving birth to walls.
                              And men
to come to understand the river gods
and to raise them trembling in the nets.
And men on the coasts and in the icy
                              mountain passes
and in all desolation.
That's right, men are needed.
                              And a song is needed.

Emerging from the depths of the night
I have come to speak of a country.
                              It so happens
poor in population.
                    But
                              it's more than that

Natural de la noche soy producto de un viaje
Dadme tiempo
                coraje
                        para hacer la canción.

Plumón de nido nivel de luna
salud del oro guitarra abierta
final de viaje donde una isla
los campesinos no tienen tierra.

Decid al viento los apellidos
de los ladrones y las cavernas
y abrid los ojos donde un desastre
los campesinos no tienen tierra.

El aire brusco de un breve puño
que se detiene junto a una piedra
abre una herida donde unos ojos
los campesinos no tienen tierra.

Los que la roban no tienen ángeles
no tienen órbita entre las piernas
no tienen sexo donde una patria
los campesinos no tienen tierra.

No tienen paz entre las pestañas
no tienen tierra no tienen tierra.

A native of the night, I am the product of a journey.
Give me time
                courage
                        to forge the song.

Feathers from a moon-high nest
health of gold a generous guitar
journey's end where an island lies
the peasants have no land.

Speak into the wind the names
of the thieves and the caves
open your eyes where a disaster lies
the peasants have no land.

The sudden swish of a brief fist
that stops moving beside the stone
opens a wound where two eyes lie
the peasants have no land.

Those who steal it have no gift
have no crown between their legs
have no sex where a country lies
the peasants have no land.

They have no peace between their eyelids,
they have no land they have no land.

País inverosímil.
                    Donde la tierra brota
y se derrama y cruje come una vena rota,
donde alcanza la estatura del vértigo,
donde las aves nadan o vuelan pero en el medio
no hay más que tierra:
                         los campesinos no tienen tierra.
Y entonces,
                    ¿de dónde ha salido esa canción?
¿Cómo es posible?
                         ¿Quién dice que entre la fina
salud del oro
                    los campesinos no tienen tierra?
Ésa es otra canción. Escuchad
la canción deliciosa de los ingenios de azúcar
y de alcohol.

Miro un brusco tropel de raíles
son del ingenio
sus soportes de verde aborigen
son del ingenio
y las mansas montañas de origen
son del ingenio
y la caña y la yerba y el mimbre
son del ingenio
y los muelles y el agua y el liquen
son del ingenio
y el camino y sus dos cicatrices
son del ingenio

Improbable country.
                        Where the earth sprouts
and spills over and cracks like a bursting vein,
where it rises to the height of frenzy,
where birds swim or fly but in between
there is only land:
                        the peasants have no land.
So then,
            where has that song come from?
How can it be?
                    Who says that among the fine
health of gold
                    the peasants have no land?
That is another song. Listen to
the delightful song of the sugar and
alcohol mills.

I see a sudden rush of rails
they belong to the company
their railroad ties of native green
belong to the company
and the gentle mountains of origin
belong to the company
and the cane and the grass and the willows
belong to the company
and the wharfs and the water and the lichen
belong to the company
and the road and its two scars
belong to the company

y los pueblos pequeños y vírgenes
son del ingenio
y los brazos del hombre más simple
son del ingenio
y sus venal de joven calibre
son del ingenio
y los guardias con voz de fusiles
son del ingenio
y las manchas de plomo en las ingles
son del ingenio
y la furia y el odio sin límites
son del ingenio
y las leyes calladas y tristes
son del ingenio
y las culpas que no se redimen
son del ingenio
veinte veces lo digo y lo dije
son del ingenio
"nuestros campos de gloria repiten"
son del ingenio
en la sombra del ancla persisten
son del ingenio
aunque arrojen la carga del crimen
lejos del puerto
con la sangre el sudor y el salitre
son del ingenio.

and the little virgin towns
belong to the company
and the limbs of the simplest man
belong to the company
and his youthful veins
belong to the company
and the guards with rifles for voices
belong to the company
and the lead stains in the groin
belong to the company
and the boundless fury and hatred
belong to the company
and the sad and silent laws
belong to the company
and the sins that are without redemption
belong to the company
twenty times I say it and I've said it
they belong to the company
"our fields upon fields of glory"
they belong to the company
in the shadow of the anchor they endure
they belong to the company
though they cast the onus of the crime
far from the port
with blood, sweat, nitrate,
they belong to the company.

Y éste es el resultado.
          El día luminoso
regresando a través de los cristales
del azúcar, primero se encuentra al labrador.
En seguida al leñero y al picador
                              de caña
rodeado de sus hijos llenando la carreta.

Y al niño del guarapo y después al anciano sereno
con el reloj, que lo mira con su muerte secreta,
y a la joven temprana cosiéndose los párpados
en el saco cien mil y al rastro del salario
perdido entre las hojas del listero. Y al perfil
sudoroso de los cargadores envueltos en su capa
de músculos morenos. Y al albañil celeste
colocando en el cielo el último ladrillo
de la chimenea. Y al carpintero gris
clavando el ataúd para la urgente muerte,
cuando suena el silbato, blanco y definitivo,
que el reposo contiene.

El día luminoso despierta en las espaldas
de repente, corre entre los raíles,
sube por las grúas, cae en los almacenes.
En los patios, al pie de una lavandera,
mojada en las canciones, cruje y rejuvenece.
En las calles se queja en el pregón. Apenas
su pie despunta desgarra los pesebres.

And this is the result.
                    The luminous day
returning across crystals
of sugar, first finds the peasant farmer.
Soon after him the woodcutter and cane
                                   cutter
surrounded by his children loading the wagon.

And the boy with the cane juice and later the serene old
man with the watch, that looks at him with its secret death,
and the young girl sewing her eyelids
into the hundred thousandth sack and the trail of wages
lost among the timekeeper's tally sheets. And the sweaty
profile of the loaders wrapped in their cloak of dark
muscles. And the celestial mason
placing in the heavens the last brick
of the chimney. And the grey carpenter
nailing together the coffin for the urgent death,
when the whistle sounds, white and final,
shrouded in repose.

The luminous day suddenly wakens
on the people's backs, runs along the rails,
climbs up the derricks, falls on the stores.
In the courtyards, at a washerwoman's feet,
it crackles soaked in songs and becomes young again.
It protests in the street vendor's cry. Scarcely
does its foot appear than it shatters cradles.

Recorre las ciudades llenas de los abogados
que no son más que placas y silencio, a los poetas
que no son más que nieblas y silencio y a los jueces
silenciosos. Sube, salta, delira en las esquinas
y el día luminoso se resuelve en un dólar inminente.

¡Un dólar! He aquí el resultado. Un borbotón de sangre.
Silenciosa, terminante. Sangre herida en el viento.
Sangre en el efectivo producto de amargura.
Éste es un país que no merece el nombre de país.
Sino de tumba, féretro, hueco o sepultura.
Es cierto que lo beso y que me besa
y que su beso no sabe más que a sangre.
Que día vendrá, oculto en la esperanza,
con su canasta llena de iras implacables
y rostros contraídos y puños y puñales.
Pero tened cuidado. No es justo que el castigo
caiga sobre todos. Busquemos los culpables.
Y entonces caiga el peso infinito de los pueblos
sobre los hombres de los culpables.

It runs through the cities filled with lawyers
who are no more than tablets and silence, with poets
who are no more than mist and silence, and the silent
judges. It climbs, jumps, raves on streetcorners
and the luminous day is transformed into an impending dollar.

A dollar! Here is the result. A torrent of blood.
Silent, terminal. Blood wounded on the wind.
Blood in the cash profit of bitterness.
This is a country unworthy of being called a country.
Call it rather tomb, coffin, hole, or sepulchre.
It is true that I kiss it and that it kisses me
and that its kiss tastes of nothing but blood.
That a day will come, hidden in hope,
its basket filled with relentless rage
and taut faces and fists and daggers.
But beware. There is no justice if the punishment
falls on everyone. Let us seek out the guilty.
And then let the infinite weight of the people
fall upon the shoulders of the guilty.

Y así
            palor de luna
                        pasajeros
despoblados y agrestes del rocío,
van montañas y valles por el río
camino de los puertos extranjeros.

Es verdad que en el tránsito del río,
cordilleras de miel, desfiladeros
de azúcar y cristales marineros
disfrutan de un metálico albedrío,

y que al pie del esfuerzo solidario
aparece el instinto proletario.
Pero ebrio de orégano y de anís

y mártir de los tórridos paisajes
hay un hombre de pie en los engranajes.
Desterrado en su tierra. Y un país
en el mundo,
                    fragrante,
                                colocado
en el mismo trayecto de la guerra.
Traficante de tierras y sin tierra.
Material. Matinal. Y desterrado.

And so
      moon-pale
           desolate
and rustic travellers of the dawn,
mountains and valleys along the river
headed toward foreign ports.

It is true that in the river's passage
mountain chains of honey, gorges
of sugar and sea crystals
enjoy a metallic free will,

and that at the base of the common effort
appears the proletarian instinct.
But drunk with oregano and anisette

and martyr to the torrid countryside
there is a man standing at the gears.
An exile in his own land. And a country
in the world,
        fragrant,
            situated
right in the path of war.
A trafficker in lands, yet landless.
Material. A dawn man. And an exile.

Y así no puede ser. Desde la sierra
procederá un rumor iluminado
probablemente ronco y derramado.
Probablemente en busca de la tierra.

Traspasará los campos y el celeste
dominio desde el este hasta el oeste
conmoviendo la última raíz

y sacando los héroes de la tumba
habrá sangre de nuevo en el país.
Habrá sangre de nuevo en el país.

And it cannot be like this. From the sierra
will come an enlightened murmur
probably harsh and scattered.
Probably in search of land.

It will go through the fields and the heavenly
sphere from east to west
stirring up the last root

and shaking the heroes from the tomb
there will again be blood in the country.
There will again be blood in the country.

Y ésta es mi última palabra.
                              Quiero
oírla. Quiero verla en cada puerta
de religión, donde una mano abierta
solicita un milagro del estero.

Quiero ver su amargura necesaria
donde el hombre y la res y el surco duermen
y adelgazan los sueños en el germen
de quietud que eterniza la plegaria.

Donde un ángel respira.
                        Donde arde
una súplica pálida y secreta
y siguiendo el carril de la carreta
un boyero se extingue con la tarde.

Después
        no quiero más que paz.
                               Un nido
de constructiva paz en cada palma.
Y quizás a propósito del alma.
el enjambre de besos
                      y el olvido.

And this is my last word.
                              I want
to hear it. I want to see it at every church
door, where an open hand
begs for a miracle from the brook.

I want to see its necessary bitterness
where man and beast and furrow sleep
and dreams become light in the bud
of quietude that prayer makes everlasting.

Where an angel breathes.
                              Where burns
a pallid, secret supplication
and following the rutted wagon tracks
an oxherd is engulfed in twilight.

Afterwards
                I want only peace.
                              A nest
of constructive peace in each palm.
And perhaps with relation to the soul
a swarm of kisses
                    and forgetfulness.

(DDW)

45

SI ALGUIEN QUIERE SABER
CUÁL ES MI PATRIA

I

Si alquien quiere saber cuál es mi patria
no la busque,
no pregunte por ella.

Siga el rastro goteante por el mapa
y su efigie de patas imperfectas.
No pregunte si viene del rocío
o si tiene espirales en las piedras
o si tiene sabor ultramarino
o si el clima le huele en primavera.
No la busque ni alargue las pupilas.
No pregunte por ella.

(¡Tanto arrojo en la lucha irremediable
y aún no hay quien lo sepa!
¡Tanto acero y fulgor de resistir
y aún no hay quien lo vea!)

No, no la busque.
Si alguien quiere saber cuál es mi patria,
no pregunte por ella.
No quiera saber si hay bosques, trinos,
penínsulas muchísimas y ajenas,
o si hay cuatro cadenas de montañas,
todas derechas,
o si hay varios destinos de bahías
y todas extranjeras.

IF ANYBODY WANTS TO KNOW
WHICH IS MY COUNTRY

I

If anybody wants to know which is my country
do not look for her,
do not ask about her.

Follow the tracks dripping on the map
and its image of imperfect paws.
Do not ask if she comes from the dew
or if she has spirals on the stones
or if she has an imported taste
or if the climate smells of her in the spring.
Do not look for her or widen your eyes.
Do not ask about her.

(So much daring in the irremediable struggle
and still there is no one who knows it!
So much steel and splendour of resistance
and still there is no one who sees it!)

No, do not look for her.
If anybody wants to know which is my country,
do not ask about her.
Do not try to know if there are forests, trills,
a multitude of far-off peninsulas,
or if there are four mountain chains,
all upright,
or if there are several destinies of bays
and all foreign.

Siga el rastro goteando pot la brisa
y allí donde la sombra se presenta,
donde el tiempo castiga y desmorona,
ya no la busque,
no pregunte por ella.
Su propia sangre, su órbita querida,
su instántineo chispazo de presencia,
su funeral de risa y de sonrisa,
su potrero de espaldas indirectas,
su puño de silencio en cada boca,
su borbotón de ira en cada mueca,
sus manos enguantadas en la fábrica y
sus pies descalzos en la carretera,
las largas cicatrices que le bajan
como antiguos riachuelos, su siniestra
figura de mujer
obligada a parir
con cada coz que busca su cadera
para echar una fila de habitantes
listos para la rueda,
todo dirá de pronto dónde existe
una patria moderna.
Dónde habrá que buscar y qué pregunta
se solicita. Porque apenas
surge la realidad y se apresura
una pregunta, ya está la respuesta.

No, no la busque.
Tendría que pelear por ella ...

Follow the tracks dripping on the breeze
and there where the shadow appears,
where time punishes and erodes,
do not look for her any longer,
do not ask about her.
Her own blood, her beloved orbit,
her instant spark of presence,
her funeral of smiles and laughter,
her pastures of winding shoulders,
her fistful of silence in each mouth,
her boiling rage in each grimace,
her gloved hands in the factory and
her bare feet on the roads,
the long scars that furrow her
like ancient streams, her fateful
figure of a woman
forced to give birth
with each kick aimed at her flank
to bring forth a row of people
ready for the rack,
everything will suddenly say where there is
a modern country.
Where the search must be and what question
must be asked. Because as soon
as reality appears and a question
is blurted out, the answer is there.

No, do not look for her.
You would have to fight for her ...

II

Así vamos los pueblos de la América
en mangas de camisa. No pregunte
nadie por la patria de nadie.
No pregunte
si el plomo está prohibido, si la sangre
está prohibida, si en las leyes
está prohibida el hambre.
Si results la noche
y firmemente los labriegos saben
el rumbo de la aurora,
el curso de la siembra. Si los sables
duermen por largo tiempo,
si están prohibidas las cárceles ...
Porque apenas un crudo mozalbete desgranado
enarbola la paz como un fragante
pabellón infinito, en nombre del amor
o de la juventud en medio de las calles,
el látigo produce su rúbrica instantánea,
su bronco privilegio. Porque apenas
un escritor coloca sus telares
en la página blanca y teje un grito
y pide paz y pide voz or pide pan y luz
para las sombras populares,
para los barrios, para las niñas,
para las fábricas, para los matorrales,
cuando no es el ostracismo es el silencio,
cuando no es el olvido es el gendarme ...

II

So we the peoples of America are going
in our shirtsleeves. Let nobody
ask about anybody's country.
Do not ask
if bullets are banned, if blood
is banned, if by law
hunger is banned.
If night falls
and the farmhands clearly know
the path of the dawn,
the course of the sowing. If the cutlasses
sleep for a long time,
if prisons are banned ...
Because no sooner does a rough wild-eyed youth
brandish peace like a fragrant
boundless banner, in the name of love
or of youth in the middle of the streets,
than the lash produces its instant flourish,
its harsh copyright. For no sooner
does a writer place his loom
upon the blank page to weave a cry
and ask for peace and for a voice or for bread and light
for people's shadows,
for neighbourhoods, for girls,
for factories, for thickets,
than it is banishment or silence,
than it is oblivion or the gendarmes ...

Y así vamos los pueblos de la América
tan numerosos y unos. No pregunte
nadie
por la patria de nadie.
Ni en los países del mar o los océanos
todos con sus hermosas capitales,
ni en las islas o los cayos
matinales.

No pregunte si hay minas infinitas,
todas inagotables,
y luchas por salvarlas del saqueo,
todas con cadaveres ...

Un aroma común, un aire justo
de familia recorre nuestros ángeles,
nuestros fusiles, nuestras metonimias ...
Un rostro amargo y una misma mano y unas tardes
melancólicas de nuestras tierras crían
los mismos sudores, los mismos ademanes
y la misma garra sangrienta y conocida.

Nadie pregunte por la patria de nadie.
Por encima de nuestras cordilleras y las líneas
fronterizas, más rejas y alambradas que carácter,
o diferencia o rumbo del perfil,
el mismo drama grande,
el mismo cerco impuro el ojo vigilante.
Veinte patrias para un solo tormento.
Un solo corazón para veinte fatigas nacionales.

And so, we the peoples of America are going
so numerous, so one. Let nobody
ask
about anybody's country.
Not in the countries of the sea or the oceans
all with their beautiful capitals,
not on the islands or the reefs
of morning.

Do not ask if there are countless mines,
all inexhaustible,
and struggles to save them from plundering,
all with corpses ...

A common scent, a very household
air passes over our angels,
our guns, our metonomies ...
A bitter face and a single hand and some sombre
evenings of our lands breed
the same sweat, the same postures,
and the same bloody and familiar claw.

Let nobody ask about anybody's country.
Above our mountain ranges and boundary
lines, more bars and barbed wire than character,
or difference or profiled course,
the same great drama,
the same lewd fence the vigilant eye.
Twenty countries for a single anguish.
A single heart for twenty national hardships.

Un mismo amor, un mismo beso para nuestras tierras
y un mismo desgarramiento en nuestra carne.

No, no pregunte
nadie por la patria de nadie.
Tendría que mudar de pensamiento
y llorar solamente por la sangre ...

A single love, a single kiss for our lands
and a single rending of our flesh.

No, let nobody
ask about anybody's country.
He would have to change his thinking
and weep solely through his blood ...

III

Si alguien quiere saber cuál es mi patria
se lo diré algún día.
Cuando hayan florecido los camellos
en medio del desierto. Cuando digan
que las mujeres bajan sus dos manos
de la cabeza y la alzan en la brisa,
cuando los trenes salgan a la calle
el día de la fiesta con sus vías
bajo el brazo y descanse el fogonero.
Cuando la caña se desnude y rían
los machetes en fuga hacia el batey
dejando en paz las manos sorprendidas.
Cuando todo milagro sea posible
y ya no sea milagro el de la vida:

Cuando empiece a bajar esta marea
de ignominia
y deje al descubierto hacia la aurora
el fondo firme de los pueblos. Día
justo de enumerar las cordilleras
y decir cuáles son las siete risas
de la nueva semana y cuáles son
los meses que contienen alegría.

Entonces se sabrá cuál es mi patria
y mucha gente irá con sus camisas
de todos los colores y ciudades.

III

If anybody wants to know which is my country
I will tell him one day.
When camels have flourished
in the middle of the desert. When they say
that women lower their hands
from their heads and raise them in the breeze,
when trains go out in the street
on holidays with their rails
under their arms, and when the fireman rests.
When the sugarcane is cut and the machetes
laugh in flight toward the clearing
leaving startled hands in peace.
When every miracle is possible and
the miracle of life is no longer a miracle:

When this tide of shame
begins to ebb
leaving the people's firm bedrock
exposed to the dawn. A good day
for counting the mountain ranges
and saying which are the seven laughters
of the new week and which are
the months that have joy in them.

Then it will be known which is my country
and the many many peoples will go with their shirts
of all colours and cities.

Llenarán sus costuras con la firma
nuestra, de nuestra libertad y entonces
irán a repartirlas.
La llevarán al viento por los valles
en todas las Antillas.

Dirán que somos libres y golosos,
que gozamos del pan y de la espiga.
Que cada hombre tiene dignidad,
cada mujer sonrisa.
Que tenemos la patria verdadera
y ésta también será la patria mía.
Si alguien quiere saber cuál es mi patria
se lo diré ese día.
Yo lo diré tocando la guitarra
con mi novia bordada en la camisa,
con botones de oro, blancos puños
y una gran amapola sonreída ...

Si alguien quiere saber dónde está ella
yo lo diré ese día.
Ahora no la busque.
No pregunte por ella todavía.

Pero el día fragante que lo sepa
procure estar bien cerca y bullicioso,
porque habrá patria grande para entonces
y no habrá ni un silencio de rodillas ...

They will fill their sewing with our
signature, with our freedom, and then
they will go out to distribute them.
They will bear them on the wind through the valleys
of all the Antilles.

They will say that we are free and sweet-toothed,
that we enjoy bread and wheat.
That every man has dignity,
every woman a smile.
That we have the true homeland
and this too will be my homeland.
If anybody wants to know which is my country
I will tell him on that day.
I will say so playing the guitar
with my sweetheart embroidered on my shirt,
with buttons of gold, white cuffs
and a great smiling poppy ...

If anybody wants to know where she is
I will tell him on that day.
Do not look for her now.
Do not ask about her yet.

But that sweet fragrant day when you know it
try to be very near and very loud,
for there will be a great country by then
and there will not be one silent man on his knees ...

IV

Si alguien quiere saber cuál es mi patria,
lo diré en una tarde americana.
Cuando el mundo se quite la cabeza
y le arranque la espina innominada.
Cuando el hilo de todas las fronteras
reja como una alfombra todas las patrias.
Y una risa inmensa
recorra las montañas
y haga huir como murciélagos despavoridos
a los acorazados con sus arrogancias,
con su larga cadena de oprobio
que une nuestras gargantas
y nos saca en sangre y pulpa
las tierras perfumadas ...

Y empiece entonces a inundar las calles
tanta gente escondida dentro de su casaca,
y las imprentas salgan a ver
con el vientre lleno de libros y de portadas
todos nuestros suburbios desde sus páginas
y las madres alcen sus hijos hacia la luz
de la aurora, sin guerra y sin amenazas ...

Día justo y solemne de contestar
de cuánto goce se compone una patria.
Cuáles son los veinte ruidos
de la nueva batalla.

IV

If anybody wants to know which is my country
I shall tell him one American evening.
When the world takes off its head
and pulls from it the nameless thorn.
When the thread of all the borders
weaves together all countries into a single rug.
And an enormous laughter
echoes through the mountains
and chases away like frightened bats
the battleships with their arrogance,
with their long chain of ignominy
that unites our throats
and strips us, our flesh and blood,
of our perfumed lands ...

And then let the streets begin to flood
with so many people hidden in their coats,
and let the presses come out to see,
their bellies filled with books and title pages,
all our slums from their pages
and let mothers hold their children up to the light
of dawn, without war and without threats ...

A just and solemn day on which to answer
of how much joy a country is composed.
Which are the twenty sounds
of the new battle.

A quién le corresponde el apetito,
a quién el gesto copioso y la guirnalda,
qué colorido el del más ancho traje,
qué ritmo el de la más noble carcajada.
Cuáles bueyes y cuáles sementales
en la exposición donde las frutas y las canastas …

Pero ahora
nadie pregunte por la patria
de nadie.

Y el día en que estalle
la libertad suprema y soberana,
procure estar bien cerca y bullicioso
porque habrá una gran patria,
una grande, inmensa, inmóvil patria para todos
y no habrá ni un país para estas lágrimas …

For whom is desire most fitting,
for whom the sweeping gesture and the garland,
of what colour the most ample gown,
of what rhythm the most noble laughter.
Which oxen and which stud bulls
in the fair with all the fruits and baskets ...

But now
let nobody ask about the country
of anybody.

And the day on which liberty
bursts forth supreme and sovereign,
try to be very close and very loud
for there will be a great country,
a great, immense, steadfast country for all
and there won't be one single country for these tears ...

(DDW)

CONTRACANTO A WALT WHITMAN

(canto a nosotros mismos)

Yo,
    un hijo del Caribe,
precisamente antillano.
Producto primitivo de una ingenua
criatura borinqueña
                        y un obrero cubano,
nacido justamente, y pobremente,
en suelo quisqueyano.
Recorrido de voces,
lleno de pupilas
que a través de las islas se dilatan,
vengo a hablarle a Walt Whitman,
un cosmos,
                un hijo de Manhattan.
Preguntarán
                ¿quién eres tú?
                            Comprendo.
Que nadie me pregunte
quién es Walt Whitman.
Iría a sollozar sobre su barba blanca.
Sin embargo,
voy a decir de nuevo quién es Walt Whitman,
un cosmos,
                un hijo de Manhattan.

COUNTERSONG TO WALT WHITMAN
(song of ourselves)

I,
   a son of the Caribbean,
Antillean to be exact.
The raw product of a simple
Puerto Rican girl
             and a Cuban worker,
born precisely, and poor,
on Quisqueyan soil.
Overflowing with voices,
full of eyes
wide open throughout the islands,
I have come to speak to Walt Whitman,
a kosmos,
        of Manhattan the son.
People will ask,
           Who are you?
                 I understand.
Nobody had better ask me
who Walt Whitman is.
I would go sob on his white beard.
And yet,
I am going to say again who Walt Whitman is,
a kosmos,
        of Manhattan the son.

Note: In the first three editions of Whitman's *Leaves of Grass,* the line in "Song of Myself" that Mir echoes here reads "Walt Whitman, an American, one of the roughs, a Kosmos," and in later editions, it reads "Walt Whitman am I, a Kosmos, of mighty Manhattan the son." The final form of the line is "Walt Whitman, a kosmos, of Manhattan the son." Mir has adapted the Spanish translation of it made by poet Léon Felipe: "*Yo, Walt Whitman, un cosmos, un hijo de Manhattan*" (literally, "I, Walt Whitman, a cosmos, a son of Manhattan") [JC].

1.

Hubo una vez un territorio puro.
Árboles y terrones sin rúbricas ni alambres.
Hubo una vez un territorio sin tacha.
Hace ya muchos años. Más allá de los padres de los padres
las llanuras jugaban a galopes de búfalos.
Las costas infinitas jugaban a las perlas.
Las rocas desceñían su vientre de diamantes.
Y las lomas jugaban a cabras y gacelas ...

Por los claros del bosque la brisa regresaba
cargada de insolencias de ciervos y abedules
que henchían de simiente los poros de la tarde.
Y era una tierra pura poblada de sorpresas.
Donde un terrón tocaba la semilla
precipitaba un bosque de dulzura fragante.
Le acometía a veces un frenesí de polen
que exprimía los álamos, los pinos, los abetos,
y enfrascaba en racimos la noche y los paisajes.
Y eran minas y bosques y praderas
cundidos de arroyuelos y nubes y animales.

1.

There once was a virgin wilderness.
Trees and land without deeds or fences.
There once was a perfect wilderness.
Many years ago. Long before the ancestors of our ancestors.
The plains would play with galloping buffalo.
The endless coastlines would play with pearls.
The rocks let loose diamonds from their wombs.
And the hills played with goats and gazelles ...

The breeze would swirl through clearings in the woods
heavy with the bold play of deer and birch trees
filling the pores of evening with seed.
And it was a virgin land filled with surprises.
Wherever a clod of earth touched a seed
all of a sudden there grew a sweet-smelling forest.
At times it was assaulted by a frenzy of pollen
squeezing out the poplars, the pines, the fir trees,
and pouring out the night and landscapes in clusters.
And there were caverns and woods and prairies
teeming with brooks and clouds and animals.

2.

(¡Oh, Walt Whitman de barba luminosa …!)
Era el ancho Far-West y el Mississippi y las Montañas
Rocallosas y el Valle de Kentucky
y las selvas de Maine y las colinas de Vermont
y el llano de las costas y más …
                              Y solamente
faltaban los delirios del hombre y su cabeza.
        Solamente faltaba que la palabra
                                        mío
penetrara en las minas y las cuevas
y cayera en el surco y besara la Estrella
Polar. Y cada hombre
                        llevara sobre el pecho,
bajo el brazo, en las pupilas y en los hombros,
su caudaloso yo,
                su permanencia
en sí mismo,
y lo volcara por aquel desenfrenado territorio.

2.

(O luminous-bearded Walt Whitman ...!)
It was the spacious Far West and the Mississippi and the Rocky
Mountains and the Valley of Kentucky
and the woods of Maine and the hills of Vermont
and the flats along the coasts and more ...
                                   And missing
were only man's fevers and his head.
       All that was missing was for the word
                              mine
to go deep inside the caverns and caves
and fall into the furrow and kiss the North
Star. And for every man
                    to carry on his chest,
under his arm, in his eyes and on his shoulders,
his abundant I,
              his permanence
in himself,
and to spill it out on that wild and savage land.

3.

Que nadie me pregunte
quién es Walt Whitman.
A través de los siglos
iría a sollozar sobre su barba blanca.
He dicho que diré
                    y estoy diciendo
quién era el infinito y luminoso Walt Whitman,
un cosmos,
¡un hijo de Manhattan!

3.

Nobody had better ask me
who Walt Whitman is.
Crossing the centuries
I would go sob on his white beard.
I have said that I will speak out
                              and I am saying
who that boundless and luminous Walt Whitman was,
a kosmos,
of Manhattan the son!

4.

Hubo una vez un intachable territorio puro.
Solamente faltaba que la palabra
                              mío
penetrara su régimen oscuro.
                      Sin embargo,
el yo que iba a decirla estaba allí
                              pero cogido
como un pez
                      en su red de costillas.
Estaba
            pero interno, pero adusto y confinado
y amaba y deshojaba sus novias amarillas.
Afuera estaba el firme sistema de la Ley.
Estaba la celosa
                      regulación de la conducta.
La Ley del algodón, la Ley del sueño,
la Ley inglesa, dura y definitiva.
                              Y apenas
un breve yo surgía entre dos párpados,
se iluminaba el cumplimiento de la Ley.
Y entonces,
cads cual derogaba su yo desestimado
entre el musgo, la sombra, la amapola
                              y el buey.

4.

There once was a perfectly virgin wilderness.
All that was missing was for the word
                                    mine
to penetrate its hidden ways.
                        And yet,
the I that was going to say it was there
                                but caught
like a fish
        in its net of ribs.
He was there
                but inside, austere and pent up
and he would love and unleaf his yellow sweethearts.
Outside was the firm system of the Law.
There was the zealous
                        rule of conduct.
The Cotton Law, the Dream Law,
the English Law, hard and definite.
                            And scarcely
a short-lived I appeared between two eyelids,
the observance of the Law was casting its light.
And then,
everyone suppressed their disparaged I
among the moss, the shade, the poppy
                            and the ox.

5.

Y un día
(¡Oh, Walt Whitman de barba insospechada ...!)
al pie de la palabra
                    yo
resplandeció la palabra
                            Democracia.
Fue un salto.
            De repente
el más recóndito yo
encontró su secreto beneficio.
Libertad de Trabajo. Libertad de Conciencia.
Libertad de Palabra. Libertad de Camino.
Libertad de aventura, proyecto y fantasía.
Libertad de fracaso, de amor y de apellido.
Libertad sin retorno ni vértices ni orugas.
Libertad de quererme y mirarme en su pupila.
Libertad de la dulce asamblea que tengo en mi corazón
contigo y con toda la infinita humanidad que rueda a través
            de todas las edades, los años, las tierras, los países,
            los credos, los horizontes ... y fue la necesaria
            instalación del júbilo.
Las colinas desataron luceros y luciérnagas.
Las uvas se embriagaron de vino y de perennidad.
En todo el territorio
se hizo la gran puerta de la oportunidad
y todo el mundo tuvo acceso a la palabra
                            mío.

5.

And one day
(O Walt Whitman of trusting beard ...!)
at the heart of the word
                    I
shined the word
                    Democracy.
It was a leap.
             All of a sudden
the most inconspicuous I
found his hidden reward.
Freedom of Work. Freedom of Conscience.
Freedom of Speech. The Open Road.
Freedom to set out, to plan ahead and to dream.
Freedom to fail, to love and to name.
Freedom with no turning back or summits or caterpillars.
Freedom to love myself and to see myself in his eye.
Freedom of the sweet assembly held in my heart
with you and with all the boundless humanity rolling through
        all the ages, the years, the lands, the countries,
            the creeds, the horizons ... and it was the
            necessary foundation of joy.
The hills unleashed bright stars and fireflies.
The grapes got drunk on wine and perennial life.
In all the land
the great door of opportunity opened
and the whole world had access to the word
                                        mine.

6.

¡Oh, Walt Whitman, tu barba sensitiva
era una red al viento!
Vibraba y se llenaba de encendidas figuras
de novias y donceles, de bravos y labriegos,
de rudos mozalbetes camino del riachuelo,
de guapos con espuelas y mozas con sonrisa,
de marchas presurosas de seres infinitos,
de trenzas o sombreros ...
Y tú fuiste escuchando
camino por camino
golpeándoles el pecho
palabra con palabra.
¡Oh, Walt Whitman de barba candorosa,
alcanzo por los años tu roja llamarada!

6.

O Walt Whitman, your sensitive beard
was a net in the wind!
It throbbed and filled with ardent figures
of sweethearts and youths, of brave souls and farmers,
of country boys walking to creeks,
of rowdies wearing spurs and maidens wearing smiles,
of the hurried marches of numberless beings,
of tresses or hats ...
And you went on listening
road after road,
striking their heartstrings
word after word.
O Walt Whitman of guileless beard,
I have come through the years to your red blaze of fire!

7.

Los hombres avanzaron con su suerte
robusta y masculina,
                    sudorosa. Pilotearon los barcos
y los días. En la ruta pelearon con los indios
y las indias. En las noches contaron sus historias
y ciudades. En la brisa colgaron sus camisas
y caminos. En los valles pusieron diligencias
y ciudades. En la brisa colgaron sus camisas
y el olor de los pechos procedentes del hacha
y a veces se extraviaron en las sombras
de un vientre de muchacha ...
Aquel territorio fue creciendo hacia arriba
y hacia abajo.
                    Rascacielos
                              y minas
se iban alejando de la tierra,
                              unidos y distantes.
Los más fuertes, los más iluminados, los más
capaces de violar un camino, fueron adelante.
Otros quedaron atrás. Pero la marcha
seguía sin sosiego, sin volver la mirada.
Era preciso
                    confianza en sí mismo.
Era preciso
              fe.
Y suavemente se forjó la canción:

7.

Men went onward with their destiny
that was robust and manly,
                              sweaty. They piloted boats
and days. On the way they fought with Indian braves
and squaws. At night they told their tales and spoke
of towns. Out on the breeze they hung their shirts
and roads. In the valleys they put their stagecoaches
and towns. Out on the breeze they hung their shirts
and the odour of their chests from swinging the axe
and sometimes they got lost in the shade
of a girl's belly ...
That land kept growing upwards
and downwards.
                Skyscrapers
                              and mines
kept leaving the earth's surface,
                                    united together and far apart.
The strongest ones, the brightest ones, the ones
most capable of blazing a trail, went onward.
Others stayed behind. But the march
went on with no rest, no looking back.
Self-confidence
                was essential.
Faith
        was essential.
And ever so gently was forged the song:

yo el cow-boy y yo el aventurero
y yo el pioneer y yo el lavador de oro
y yo Alvin, yo William con mi nombre y mi suerte
                    de barajas,
y yo el predicador con mi voz de barítono
y yo la doncella que tengo mi cara
y yo la meretriz que tengo mi contorno
y yo el comerciante, capitán de mi plata
y yo
            el ser humano
en pos de la fortuna para mí, sobre mí,
detrás de mí.
              Y con el mundo entero
a mis pies, sometido a mi voz,
recogido en mi espalda
          y la estatura de la cordillera yo
          y las espigas de la llanura yo
          y el resplandor de los arados yo
          y las orillas de los arroyos yo
          y el corazón de la amatista yo
y yo
       ¡Walt Whitman,
                  un cosmos,
       un hijo de Manhattan …!

I the cowboy and I the adventurer
and I the pioneer and I the gold panner
and I Alvin, I William with my name and my luck
        at cards,
and I the preacher with my baritone voice
and I the maiden who have my face
and I the prostitute who have my figure
and I the merchant, captain of my silver
and I
        the human being
in pursuit of fortune for myself, above me,
behind me.
                And with the whole world
at my feet, subject to my voice,
gathered at my back
        and the heights of the mountain range I
        and the wheat of the prairie I
        and the glint of the plows I
        and the banks of the streams I
        and the heart of the amethyst I
and I
        Walt Whitman,
                        a kosmos,
        of Manhattan the son ...!

8.

¡Secreta maravilla de una historia que nace ...!
Con aquel ancho grito
fue construida una nación gigante.
Formada de relatos y naciones pequeñas
que entonces se encontraban como el mundo
entre dos grandes mares ...
                              Y luego
se ha llenado de golfos, islotes y ballenas,
esclavos, argonautas y esquimales ...
Por los mares bravíos
empezó a transitar el clíper yanqui,
en tierra se elevaron estructuras de acero,
se escribieron poemas y códigos y mírmoles
y aquella nación obtuvo sus ardientes batallas
y sus fechas gloriosas y sus heroes totales
que tenían aún entre los labios
                              la fragancia
y el zumo
          de la tierra olorosa con que hacían su pan,
                su trayecto y su equipaje ...
Y aquélla fue una gran nación de rumbos y albedrío.
Y el yo
          — la rotación de todos los espejos
sobre una sola imagen —
halló su prodigioso mensaje primitivo
en un inmenso, puro, territorio intachable
que lloraba la ausencia de la palabra
                mío.

8.

Secret wonder of a history being born ...!
With that ample cry
a giant nation was built.
Made out of tall tales and small nations
that were then, like the world,
between two great seas ...

                         And soon
it filled with gulfs, islands and whales,
slaves, Argonauts and Eskimos ...
The Yankee clipper
began to sail the wild seas,
on land steel structures were erected,
poems and codes and marble statues were inscribed
and that nation obtained its fierce battles
and its glorious dates and its perfect heroes
who still had on their lips

                        the fragrance
and the sap
        of the sweet-smelling land with which they made
            their bread, their journey and their gear ...
And that was a great nation of pathways and free will.
And the I
        — the revolving of all mirrors
around a single image —
found its sprawling primitive message
in an immense, perfectly virgin land
that wept over the absence of the word
            mine.

9.

Porque
    ¿qué ha sido un gran poeta indeclinable
      sino un estanque límpido
        donde un pueblo descubre su perfecto
          semblante?
¿Qué ha sido
      sino un parque sumergido
        donde todos los hombres se reconocen
        por el lenguaje?
¿Y qué
    sino una cuerda de infinita guitarra
      donde pulsan los dedos de los pueblos
        su sencilla, su propia, su fuerte y
         verdadera canción innumerable?
Por eso tú, numeroso Walt Whitman, que viste y
    deliraste
la palabra precisa para cantar tu pueblo,
que en medio de la noche dijiste
                 yo
y el pescador se comprendió en su capa
y el cazador se oyó en mitad de su disparo
y el leñador se conoció en su hacha
y el labriego en su siembra y el lavador
de oro en su semblante amarillo sobre el agua
y la doncella en su ciudad futura
              que crece y que madura
bajo la saya

9.

For

    what has a great undeniable poet been
       but a crystal-clear pool
          where a people discover their perfect
           likeness?

What has he been
       but a deep garden
          where all men recognize themselves
           through language?

And what
      but the chord of a boundless guitar
         where the fingers of the people play
           their simple, their own, their strong and
             true, innumerable song?

For that's why you, numerous Walt Whitman, who saw
    and ranted
just the right word for singing your people,
who in the middle of the night said
               I
and the fisherman understood himself in his slicker
and the hunter heard himself in the midst of his gunshot
and the woodcutter recognized himself in his axe
and the farmer in his freshly sown field and the gold
panner in his yellow reflection on the water
and the maiden in her future town
               growing and maturing
under her skirt

y la meretriz en su fuente de alegría
y el minero de sombra en sus pasos debajo de la patria ...
cuando el alto predicador, bajando la cabeza,
entre dos largas manos, decía
                              yo
y se encontraba unido al fundidor y al vendedor
y al caminante oscuro de suave polvareda
y al soñador y al trepador
y al albañil terrestre parecido a una lápida
y al labrador y al tejedor
y al marinero blanco parecido a un pañuelo ...
Y el pueblo entero se miraba a sí mismo
cuando escuchaba la palabra
                              yo
y el pueblo entero se escuchaba en ti mismo
cuando escuchaba la palabra
                              yo, Walt Whitman, un cosmos,
                              ¡un hijo de Manhattan ...!
Porque tú eras el pueblo, tú eras yo,
and yo era la Democracia, el apellido del pueblo,
y yo era también Walt Whitman, un cosmos,
¡un hijo de Manhattan ...!

and the prostitute in her fountain of gaiety
and the miner of darkness in his steps beneath his homeland ...
When the tall preacher, bowing his head
between his two long hands, said

I

and found himself united with the foundryman and the salesman
with the obscure traveller in a soft cloud of dust
with the dreamer and the climber,
with the earthy mason resembling a stone slab,
with the farmer and the weaver,
with the sailor in white resembling a handkerchief ...
And all the people saw themselves
when they heard the word

I

and all the people heard themselves in your song
when they heard the word

I, Walt Whitman, a kosmos,
of Manhattan the son ...!

Because you were the people, you were I,
and I was Democracy, the people's family name,
and I was also Walt Whitman, a kosmos,
of Manhattan the son ...!

10.

Nadie supo qué noche desgreñada,
un rostro frío, de bajo celentéreo,
se halló en una moneda. Qué reseco semblante
se pareció de pronto a un círculo metálico y sonoro.
Qué cara seca se vio en circulación de mano en mano.
Qué seca boca dijo de pronto
                              yo
y empezó a conjugarse a cumplirse y a multiplicarse
en todas las monedas.
En monedas de oro, de cobre, de níquel,
en monedas de manos, de venas de vírgenes,
de labradores y pastores, de cabreros y albañiles.
Nadie supo quién fue el desceñido primero.
Mas se le vio una mañana adquirir el crepúsculo.
Mas se le vio otra mañana comprar la conciencia.
Y del fondo de los ríos, de los barrancos, de la médula
de los arbustos, del filo de las cordilleras,
pasando por torrentes de sudor y de sangre,
surgieron entonces los Bancos, los Trusts, los monopolios,
las Corporaciones ... Y, cuando nadie lo supo,
fueron a dar allí la cara de la niña y el corazón
del aventurero y las cabriolas del cow-boy y los anhelos
del pioneer ... y todo aquel inmenso territorio

10.

Nobody knew on what dishevelled night,
a cold visage, of some low spineless creature,
appeared on a coin. What shrivelled up likeness
suddenly turned into a loud, round piece of metal.
What dry face was seen passing from hand to hand.
What dry mouth suddenly said

I

and began to fit in, to fulfill itself and to multiply
on all the coins.
On coins made of gold, of copper, of nickel,
on coins made of hands, of veins of virgins,
of farmers and shepherds, of goatherds and masons.
Nobody knew who was the first one to be let loose.
But one morning he was seen acquiring the dawn.
But one morning he was seen buying a conscience.
And from the depths of the rivers, from the ravines, from the pith
of the underbrush, from the ridges of the mountain ranges,
passing through torrents of sweat and blood,
the Banks, the Trusts, the monopolies, the Corporations
all, sprang up ... And, when nobody knew it,
the face of the little girl and the heart
of the adventurer and the cavorting of the cowboy and the longings
of the pioneer ended up there ... and that whole immense land

empezó a circular por las cajas de los Bancos, los libros
de las Corporaciones, las oficinas de los rascacielos,
las máquinas de calcular …
                        y ya:
se le vio una mañana adquirir la gran puerta de la oportunidad
y ya más nadie tuvo acceso a la palabra mío
y ya más nadie ha comprendido la palabra yo.

began to circulate through the vaults of the Banks, the books
of the Corporations, the offices of the skyscrapers,
the calculating machines ...
                              And then, finally:
one morning he was seen acquiring the great door of opportunity
and since then nobody has had access to the word mine
and since then nobody has understood the word I.

11.

Preguntadlo a la noche y al vino y a la aurora ...
Por detrás de las colinas de Vermont, los llanos de las Costas,
por el ancho Far-West y las Montañas Rocallosas,
por el valle de Kentucky y las selvas de Maine.
Atravesad las fábricas de muebles y automóviles, los muelles,
las minas, las casas de apartamientos, los ascensores celestiales,
los lupanares, los instrumentos de los artistas;
buscad un piano oscuro, revolved las cuerdas,
los martillos, el teclado, rompedle el arpa silenciosa
y tiradla sobre los últimos raíles de la madrugada ...
Inútilmente.
No encontraréis el limpio acento de la palabra
                                                        yo.
Quebrad un teléfono y un disco de baquelita,
arrancadle los alambres a un altoparlante nocturno,
sacad al sol alma de un violín Stradivarius ...
Inútilmente.
No encontraréis el limpio acento de la palabra
                                                        yo.
(¡Oh, Walt Whitman, de barba desgarrada!)
¡Qué de rostros caídos, qué de lenguas atadas,
qué de vencidos hígados y arterias derrotadas ...!
No encontraréis
                más nunca
                                        el acento sin mancha
de la palabra
                yo.

11.

Ask the night and the wine and the dawn about it ...
Out around the hills of Vermont, the flats along the coasts,
throughout the spacious Far West and the Rocky Mountains,
throughout the Valley of Kentucky and the woods of Maine.
Go through the furniture and automobile plants, the docks,
the mines, the apartment houses, the celestial elevators,
the brothels, the instruments of artists;
look for an obscure piano, pull apart the chords,
the hammers, the keyboard, break its silent harp
and cast it upon the last rails of the dawn ...
No use.
You won't find the pure sound of the word
                                                    I.

Smash a telephone and a phonograph record,
tear out the wires from a loudspeaker at night,
take the soul of a Stradivarius out into the sun ...
No use.
You won't find the pure sound of the word
                                                    I.

(O Walt Whitman, of tattered beard!)
What about the fallen faces, what about the silenced tongues,
what about the defeated guts and the ruined arteries ...!
You won't find
                    anymore
                                    the flawless sound
of the word
            I.

Ahora,
      escuchadme bien:
si alguien quiere encontrar de nuevo
la antigua palabra
        yo
vaya a la calle del oro, vaya a Wall Street.
No preguntéis por Mr. Babbitt. Él os lo dirá.
— Yo, Babbitt, un cosmos,
un hijo de Manhattan.
          Él os lo dirá
— Traedme las Antillas
sobre varios calibres presurosos, sobre cintas
de ametralladoras, sobre los caterpillares de los tanques
traedme las Antillas.
        Y en medio de un aroma silencioso
        allá viene la isla de Santo Domingo.
— Traedme la América Central.
        Y en medio de un aroma pavoroso
        allá viene callada Nicaragua.
— Traedme la América del Sur.
        Y en medio de un aroma pesaroso
        allá viene cojeando Venezuela.
        Y en medio de un celeste bogotazo
        allá viene cayendo Colombia.
Allá viene cayendo Ecuador.
Allá viene cayendo Brasil.
Allá viene cayendo Puerto Rico.

12.

Now,
      listen to me carefully:
if any of you wants to find again
the old word
         I
go to the street paved with gold, go to Wall Street.
Don't bother asking Mr. Babbitt. He'll only tell you:
"I, Babbitt, a kosmos,
of Manhattan the son."
              He'll only tell you:
"Bring me the Antilles
on several rapid-fire calibres, on machine-gun
belts, on the caterpillar treads of tanks
bring me the Antilles."
                 And in the midst of a silent aroma
          here comes the island of Santo Domingo.
"Bring me Central America."
                 And in the midst of a frightening aroma
          here comes Nicaragua silenced.
"Bring me South America."
                 And in the midst of a gloomy aroma
          here comes Venezuela limping.
                 And in the midst of a heavenly ruin
          here comes Colombia falling.
          Here comes Ecuador falling.
          Here comes Brazil falling.
          Here comes Puerto Rico falling.

En medio de un volumen salino
allá viene cayendo Chile ...
Vienen todos. Allá vienen cayendo.
Cuba trae su dolor envuelto en un estremecimiento de comparsas.
México trae su rencor envuelto en una sola mirada fronteriza.
Y Haití, y Uruguay y Paraguay, vienen cayendo.
Y Guatemala, El Salvador y Panamá, vienen cayendo.
Vienen todos. Vienen cayendo.
No preguntéis por Mr. Babbitt, os lo he dicho.
— Traedme todos esos pueblos en azúcar, en nitrato,
en estaño, en petróleo, en bananas,
                                        en almíbar
traedme todos esos pueblos.
No preguntéis por Mr. Babbitt, os lo he dicho.
Vienen todos, vienen cayendo.

In the midst of a salty mass
here comes Chile falling ...
They all come. Here they come falling.
Cuba brings her grief wrapped in a shudder of masquerades.
Mexico brings her rancour wrapped in a single border glance.
And Haiti, and Uruguay and Paraguay, they come falling.
And Guatemala, El Salvador and Panama, they come falling.
They all come. They come falling.
Don't bother asking Mr. Babbitt, I'm warning you.
"Bring me all those nations in sugar, in nitrate,
in tin, in oil, in bananas,

in syrup
bring me all those nations."
Don't bother asking Mr. Babbitt, I'm warning you.
They all come, they come falling.

13.

Si queréis encontrar el duro acento moderno
de la palabra
                yo
                        id a Santo Domingo.
Pasad por Nicaragua. Preguntad en Honduras.
Escuchad al Perú, a Bolivia, a la Argentina.
Dondequiera hallaréis un capitán sonoro
                                        un yo.
Un jefe luminoso,
                        un yo, un cosmos.
Un hombre providencial,
                        un yo, un cosmos, un hijo de su patria.
Y en medio de la noche fragorosa de la América
escucharéis, detrás de madureces y fragancias,
mezclados con sordos quejidos, con blasfemias y
                        gritos,
con sollozos y puños, con largas lágrimas y largas
aristas y maldiciones largas
                        un yo, Walt Whitman, un cosmos,
                        un hijo de Manhattan.
Una canción antigua convertida en razón de fuerza
entre los engranajes de las factorías, en las calles
de las ciudades. Un yo, un cosmos, en las guardarrayas,
y en los vagones y en los molinos de los centrales.
Una canción antigua convertida en razón de sangre
                y de miseria,
un yo, un Walt Whitman, un cosmos,
¡un hijo de Manhattan ...!

98

13.

If you want to find the harsh modern sound
of the word

      I

          go to Santo Domingo.
Pass through Nicaragua. Ask around in Honduras.
Listen to Peru, to Bolivia, to Argentina.
Everywhere you will run into a high-sounding captain

                              an I.

A shining leader,

         an I, a kosmos.
A God-sent man,

         an I, a kosmos, son of his homeland.
And in the middle of the deafening night of America
you will hear, behind ripe things and sweet smells,
mixed with faint moans, swearwords and

         shouts,
with sobs and fists, with long tears and long
bristles and long curses

         an I, Walt Whitman, a kosmos,
         of Manhattan the son.
An old song turned into the song of force
among the gears of the factories, in the streets
of the cities. An I, a kosmos, in the cane fields,
and in the railroad cars and the sugar mills.
An old song turned into the song of blood

         and of misery,
an I, a Walt Whitman, a kosmos,
of Manhattan the son ...!

Porque
    ¿qué ha sido la ventura de los pueblos
        si no un cambio continuo, un movimiento eterno,
            un fuego infinito que se enciende y que se apaga?
¿Qué ha sido
    si no un chorro incontenido,
        espejo ayer de oteros y palmares,
            hoy nube blanca?
¿Y qué
    si no una brega infatigable
        en que hoy manda un puñado de golosos
        y mañana los puños deliciosos,
            fragantes y frenéticos del pueblo
            innumerable?
Por eso tú, innúmero Walt Whitman,
que en mitad de la noche dijiste
                yo
y el herrero sonoro se descubrió en la llama
y el forjador y el fogonero
y el cuidador del faro, celeste de miradas,
y el fundidor y el leñero
y la niña celeste colando la alborada
y el pionero y el bombero
y el cochero y el aventurero y el arriero ...

For
    what has been the fate of nations
        if not constant change, eternal movement,
            a quenchless fire that flares up and fades?
What has it been
    if not a free-flowing stream,
        yesterday a mirror of knolls and palm groves,
           today a white cloud?
And what
    if not a never-ending struggle
        dominated today by a handful of greedy gluttons
           and tomorrow by the delicious, fragrant
               and furious hands of the innumerable
               people?
For that reason you, numberless Walt Whitman,
who in the middle of the night said
               I
and the clanging blacksmith discovered himself in his flame
and the smelter and the stoker
and the lighthouse keeper, of heavenly gazes,
and the foundryman and the lumberjack
and the heavenly girl straining the dawn
and the pioneer and the fireman
and the coachman and the adventurer and the mule driver ...

Tú
            que en medio de la noche dijiste
                Yo, Walt Whitman, un cosmos,
                un hijo de Manhattan
y un pueblo entero se descubrió en tu lengua
y se lanzó de lleno a construir su casa,
hoy,
            que ha perdido su casa,
hoy,
            que tiene un puñado de golosos sonrientes y
                engreídos,
hoy,
            que ha cambiado el fuego infinito que se enciende
                y que se apaga
hoy …
hoy no te reconoce
                desgarrado Walt Whitman,
porque tu signo está guardado en las cajas de los Bancos,
porque tu voz está en las islas guardadas por arrecifes
            de bayonetas y puñales,
porque tu voz inunda los decretos y los centros de Beneficencia
y los juegos de lotería,
porque hoy,
                cuando un magnate sonrosado,
en medio de la noche cósmica,
desenfrenadamente dice
                        yo

You,
>who in the middle of the night said,
>>I, Walt Whitman, a kosmos
>>of Manhattan the son
and an entire people discovered themselves in your tongue
and all rushed full tilt into building their house,
today,
>when they have lost their house,
today,
>when among them are a handful of smiling, spoiled
>>gluttons,
today
>when the quenchless fire that flares up and fades
>>has changed
today ...
today the people do not recognize you
>>>>tattered Walt Whitman,
because your sign is locked up in the vaults of the Banks,
because your voice is on islands guarded by reefs of
>bayonets and daggers,
because your voice floods the decrees and the Welfare Centers
and the lotteries,
because today,
>>when a rosy-cheeked tycoon
in the middle of the cosmic night
wantonly says
>>I

detrás de su garganta se escucha el ruido de la muchedumbre
ensangrentadas exploradas refugiadas
que torvamente dicen
                    tú
y escupen sangre entre los engranajes,
en las fronteras y las guardarrayas …
¡Oh, Walt Whitman de barba interminable!

behind his throat resounds the clamour of the masses
bloodstained exploited refugees
who furiously are saying
                    you
and spitting blood among the gears,
on the borders and in the cane fields ...
O Walt Whitman of never-ending beard!

Y ahora
ya no es la palabra
                    yo
la palabra cumplida
la palabra de toque para empezar el mundo.
Y ahora
ahora es la palabra
                    nosotros.
Y ahora,
ahora es llegada la hora del contracanto.
        Nosostros los ferroviarios,
        nosotros los estudiantes,
        nosotros los mineros,
        nosotros los campesinos,
        nosotros los pobres de la tierra,
        los pobladores del mundo,
        los héroes del trabajo cotidiano,
        con nuestro amor y con nuestros puños,
        enamorados de la esperanza.
        Nosotros los blancos,
        los negros, los amarillos,
        los indios, los cobrizos,
        los moros y morenos,
        los rojos y aceitunados,
        los rubios y los platinos,
        unificados por el trabajo,

15.

And now
it is no longer the word

        I

the accomplished word
the password to begin the world.
And now
now it is the word

        we.

And now,
now has come the hour of the countersong.
    We the railroad workers,
    we the students,
    we the miners,
    we the peasants,
    we the wretched of the earth,
    the populators of the world,
    the heroes of everyday work,
    with our love and our fists,
    enamoured of hope.
    We the white-skinned,
    the black-skinned, the yellow-skinned,
    the Indians, the copper-skinned,
    the Moors and dark-skinned,
    the red-skinned and olive-skinned,
    the blonds and platinum blonds,
    united by work,

por la miseria, por el silencio,
por el grito de un hombre solitario
que en medio de la noche,
con un perfecto látigo,
con un salario oscuro,
con un puñal de oro y un semblante de hierro,
desenfrenadamente grita

        yo

y siente el eco cristalino
de una ducha de sangre
que decididamente se alimenta en

         nosotros

y en medio de los muelles alejándose

         nosotros

y al pie del horizonte de las fábricas

         nosotros

y en la flor y en los cuadros y en los túneles

         nosotros

y en la alta estructura camino de las órbitas

         nosotros

camino de los mármoles

         nosotros

camino de las cárceles

         nosotros ...

by misery, by silence,
by the cry of a solitary man
who in the middle of the night,
with a perfect whip,
with a meagre wage,
with a gold dagger and an iron face,
wildly cries out
                    I
and hears the crystal-clear echo
of a shower of blood
that relentlessly feeds on us
                                        ourselves
among the docks receding in the distance
                                        ourselves
below the skyline of the factories
                                        ourselves
in the flower, in the pictures, in the tunnels
                                        ourselves
in the tall structure on the way to orbits
                                        ourselves
on the way to marble halls
                                        ourselves
on the way to prisons
                                ourselves ...

Y un día,
en medio del asombro más grande de la historia,
pasando a través de muros y murallas
la risa y la victoria,
encendiendo candiles de júbilo en los ojos
y en los túneles y en los escombros,
¡oh, Walt Whitman de barba nuestra y definitiva!
Nosotros para nosotros, sobre nosotros
y delante de nosotros ...
Recogeremos puños y semilleros de todos los pueblos
y en carrera de hombros y brazos reunidos
los plantaremos repentinamente
en las calles de Chile, de Ecuador y Colombia,
de Perú y Paraguay,
de El Salvador y Brasil,
en los suburbios de Buenos Aires y de La Habana
y allá en Macorís del Mar, pueblo pequeño y mío,
hondo rincón de aguas perdido en el Caribe,
donde la sangre tiene
cierto rumor de hélices quebrándose en el río ...

16.

And one day,
amid the greatest shock in history,
scaling walls and ramparts,
laughter and victory,
lighting lamps of jubilation in eyes
and in tunnels and on rubble,
— O Walt Whitman of our ultimate beard!
We for ourselves, upon ourselves
and ahead of ourselves ...
We will gather fists and seedlings from all our nations
and in a rush of linked arms and shoulders
all of a sudden we will plant them
in the streets of Chile, of Ecuador and Colombia,
of Peru and Paraguay,
of El Salvador and Brazil,
in the suburbs of Buenos Aires and Havana
and there in Macorís del Mar, my own small town,
a water-bound corner lost out in the Caribbean,
where blood
sounds like propeller blades breaking in the river ...

¡Oh, Walt Whitman de estampa proletaria!
Por las calles de Honduras y el Uruguay.
Por los campos de Haití y los rumbos de Venezuela.
En plena Guatemala con su joven espiga.
En Costa Rica y en Panamá.
En Bolivia, en Jamaica y dondequiera,
dondequiera que un hombre de trabajo
se trague la sonrisa,
se muerda la mirada,
escupa la garganta silenciosa
en la faz del fusil y del jornal.
¡Oh, Walt Whitman!
Blandiendo el corazón de nuestros días delante de nosotros,
nosotros y nosotros y nosotros.

O Walt Whitman of proletarian stamp!
Through the streets of Honduras and Uruguay.
Through the fields of Haiti and on the paths of Venezuela.
Deep in Guatemala with its young corn.
In Costa Rica and in Panama.
In Bolivia, in Jamaica and anywhere,
anywhere a working man
swallows his smile,
bites on his gaze,
spits from his silenced throat
in the face of a gun and a miserable day's wage.
O Walt Whitman!
Brandishing the heart of the days we have ahead of ourselves,
ourselves and ourselves and ourselves.

¿Por qué queríais escuchar a un poeta?
Estoy hablando con unos y con otros.
Con aquellos que vinieron a apartarlo de su pueblo,
a separarlo de su sangre y de su tierra,
a inundarle su camino.
Aquellos que lo inscribieron en el ejército.
Los que violaron su barba luminosa y le pusieron un fusil
sobre sus hombros cargados de doncellas y pioneros.
Los que no quieren a Walt Whitman el demócrata,
sino a un tal Whitman atómico y salvaje.
Los que quieren ponerle zapatones
para aplastar la cabeza de los pueblos.
Moler en sangre las sienes de las niñas.
Desintegrar en átomos las fibras del abuelo.
Los que toman la lengua de Walt Whitman
por signo de metrella,
por bandera de fuego.
¡No, Walt Whitman, aquí están los poetas de hoy
levantados para justificarte!
" — *¡Poetas venideros, levantaos, porque vosotros debéis justificarme!*"
Aquí estamos, Walt Whitman, para justificarte.
Aquí estamos
        por ti
              pidiendo paz.
La paz que requerías
para empujar el mundo con tu canto.

17.

Why did you want to listen to a poet?
I am speaking to one and all.
To those of you who came to isolate him from his people,
to separate him from his blood and his land,
to flood his road.
Those of you who drafted him into the army.
The ones who defiled his luminous beard and put a gun
on his shoulders that were loaded with maidens and pioneers.
Those of you who do not want Walt Whitman, the democrat,
but another Whitman, atomic and savage.
The ones who want to outfit him with boots
to crush the heads of nations.
To grind into blood the temples of little girls.
To smash into atoms the old man's flesh.
The ones who take the tongue of Walt Whitman
for a sign of spraying bullets,
for a flag of fire.
No, Walt Whitman, here are the poets of today
aroused to justify you!
"Poets to come! ... Arouse! for you must justify me."
Here we are, Walt Whitman, to justify you.
Here we are
        for your sake
                demanding peace.
The peace you needed
to drive the world with your song.

Aquí estamos
   salvando tus colinas de Vermont,
tus selvas de Maine, el zumo y la fragancia de tu tierra,
tus guapos con espuelas, tus mozas con sonrisas,
tus rudos mozalbetes camino del riachuelo.
Salvándolos, Walt Whitman, de los traficantes
que toman tu lenguaje por lenguaje de guerra.
¡No, Walt Whitman, aquí están los poetas de hoy,
los obreros de hoy, los pioneros de hoy, los campesinos
de hoy,
   firmes y levantados para justificarte!
¡Oh, Walt Whitman de barba levantada!
Aquí estamos sin barba,
sin brazos, sin oído,
sin fuerzas en los labios,
mirados de reojo,
rojos y perseguidos,
llenos de pupilas
que a través de las islas se dilatan,
llenos de coraje, de nudos de soberbia
que a través de los pueblos se desatan,
con tu signo y tu idioma de Walt Whitman
aquí estamos
   en pie
    para justificarte,
¡continuo compañero de Manhattan!

Here we are
        saving your hills of Vermont,
your woods of Maine, the sap and fragrance of your land,
your spurred rowdies, your smiling maidens,
your country boys walking to creeks.
Saving them, Walt Whitman, from the tycoons
who take your language for the language of war.
No, Walt Whitman, here are the poets of today,
the workers of today, the pioneers of today, the peasants
of today,
        firm and roused to justify you!
O Walt Whitman of aroused beard!
Here we are without beards,
without arms, without ears,
without any strength in our lips,
spied on,
red and persecuted,
full of eyes
wide open throughout the islands,
full of courage, of knots of pride
untied through all the nations,
with your sign and your language, Walt Whitman,
here we are
        standing up
           to justify you,
our constant companion of Manhattan!

(JC)

117

AL PORTAVIONES *INTRÉPIDO*

Santo Domingo, febrero de 1962 (de las agencias cablegráficas internacionales): "Mil quinientos marinos del portaviones *Intrépid* desembarcaron aquí en viaje de descanso y esparcimiento."

Yo sé que eres un triunfo de formidable acero,

yo sé que tus marinos son muchos abejorros
blancos de nudoso pañuelo,

yo sé que por la línea que ronda tu cintura
de hierro vaga una lengua azul
que lame y acaricia tus entrañas de fuego,

yo sé que por las ondas que muerden tus dos hélices
huyen despavoridos los tiburones y los celentéreos,

yo sé que cuando suenan tus públicos cañones
huyen como palomas o gallaretas los archipiélagos;

yo sé que eres un portaviones todopoderoso,

yo sé que tú defiendes un formidable imperio
que se reclina bajo tus hombros,
que en ti se apoya y extiende su comercio,

TO THE AIRCRAFT CARRIER *INTREPID*

(Santo Domingo, February 1962 (from the international cable agencies): "Fifteen thousand sailors landed here from the U.S.S. aircraft carrier *Intrepid* on a tour of rest and recreation."

I know you are a triumph of formidable steel,

I know that your sailors are so many beetles,
in white with knotted scarves,

I know that along the line that circles your iron
waist wanders a blue tongue
that licks and hugs your iron bowels,

I know that through the waves bitten by your two propellers
sharks and sea serpents flee in terror,

I know that when your public cannons boom
archipelagos flee like doves or coots;

I know you are an all-powerful aircraft carrier,

I know that you defend a formidable empire
that reclines beneath your shoulders,
that leans upon you and extends its commerce,

yo sé que eres un portaviones todopoderoso,
un dios marino que vomita fuego
y hunde de un solo soplo las pequeñas Antillas
como todo un poderoso portaviones *Intrépido.*

Pero tú has ido a la pequeña rada de Santo Domingo,
pero tú has ido a la dulce bahía de Santo Domingo
ligeramente agitada por ondas subterráneas
en los alrededores de este mes de febrero,

pero tú has ido a la dulce bahía de Santo Domingo
con todos tus marinos de nudoso pañuelo,
pero tú has ido a las pequeñas aguas de Santo Domingo
solamente por miedo,
solamente por miedo.

A estas aguas pacíficas y elásticas,
solamente por miedo.

¡Quien pudiera decirlo de tus bronces,
portaviones *Intrépido*!
Tú tan lleno de potencias interiores,
tú tan lleno de bruscas erupciones
y movimientos sísmicos
y huracanes de roca derretida
y tanto fuego,
capaz de aniquilar a todas las Antillas
con un solo resuello,
surto en la enternecida rada de Santo Domingo
solamente por miedo,

I know you are an all-powerful aircraft carrier,
a sea god that vomits fire
and sinks with a single puff the little Antilles
like an almighty aircraft carrier *Intrepid.*

But you have gone to the tiny roadstead of Santo Domingo,
but you have gone to the gentle bay of Santo Domingo
gently stirred by subterranean waves
in the environs of this month of February,

but you have gone to the gentle bay of Santo Domingo,
with all your sailors with their knotted scarves,
but you have gone to the backwaters of Santo Domingo,
out of fear,
out of fear.

To these pacific and elastic waters,
out of fear.

Who could've said it of your bronze,
carrier *Intrepid!*
You so filled with inner powers,
so filled with brusque eruptions
and seismic movements
and hurricanes of molten rock
and so much fire,
able to annihilate all the Antilles
with a single puff,
anchored in the gentle roadstead of Santo Domingo
out of fear,

con todos tus cañones desplazados
solamente por miedo,
bien ceñido el feroz cinturón acorazado
solamente por miedo.

¿Será porque la carabela capitana,
aquella Santa María, hace ya mucho tiempo,
vino a amarrar indígenas después de descubiertos
y fue en los farallones y las rocas
convertida en cadáver marinero?

¿Será porque el furioso buque insignia
acorazado de Memphis, no hace aún mucho tiempo,
vino con sus cuatro chimeneas
a contener al pueblo
y fue en los farallones y las rocas
convertido en cadáver marinero?

No, portaviones *Intrépido*,
tú eres demasiado triunfo
de la alianza del bronce y el acero
para huir de farallones y de rocas,
de la espuma y del viento,

a ti te aterrorizan otras fuerzas
más anchas que el imperio
que apenas se cobija en tu coraza
como los celentéreos,
que ponen en peligro tu sendero
y espantan tu comercio,

with all your cannons displaced
out of fear,
well girt the fiercely armoured belt
out of fear.

Can it be because the flagship caravel,
that *Santa María,* now so long ago,
came to tie up Indians once they were discovered
and was turned into a marine corpse
on the cliffs and rocks?

Can it be because the furious armoured pennant
ship *Memphis,* now not so long ago,
came with its four smokestacks
to hold down the people
and was turned into a marine corpse
on the cliffs and rocks?

No carrier *Intrepid,*
you are too much the triumph
of the wedding of bronze and steel
to flee from cliffs and rocks,
foam and wind,

other forces terrify you
wider than the empire
that is scarcely protected in your armour
like jelly fish,
forces that endanger your course
and frighten your commerce,

a ti te aterrorizan estos hombres,
fieros y subterráneos,
que de pronto crecen, se dan la mano
por todos los países,
rompen gobiernos como si fueran viejas
cartas marcadas o portaviones viejos,
suben y destruyen las mentiras
de todos los imperios,
de todas las agencias cablegráficas,
de todos los consorcios extranjeros,
de todos los cañones y los buques
soberbios, de todos los aviones
y de los portaviones,
los aviadores y los marineros,
las embajadas y los consulados,
de todos los Estados y sus Departamentos,
sus Congresos y sus Conferencias,
su diplomacia y sus testaferros.

A ti te atemorizan esas ganas
de morirse que tienen estos pueblos,
porque van muchos años, muchas elecciones,
muchos millones y muchos prisoneros
y muchos jornadas de sudor no pagado
y demasiado silencio,
y con esto no pueden tus cañones de bronce,
tu coraza de acero,
y con esto no pueden tus mentiras de plomo,
tus entrañas de fuego,

these men terrify you,
fierce and subterranean,
who suddenly increase, clasp hands
across all countries,
smash governments as if they were old
marked cards or aircraft carriers,
who rise up and destroy the lies
of all the empires,
all the cable offices,
all the foreign syndicates,
all the cannons and proud
ships, all the aircraft
and aircraft carriers,
the aviators and sailors,
the embassies and consulates,
all the States and their Departments,
their Congresses and their Conferences,
their diplomacy and their figureheads.

You are frightened by the longing
to die among these people,
for many years have gone by, many elections,
many millions and many prisoners
and many workdays of unpaid sweat
and too much silence,
and this is too much for your bronze cannons,
your steel armour-plate,
too much for your leaden lies,
your fiery bowels,

porque van muchos años, mucha sangre
mezclada con sudores y atropellos,
mucha mutilación y mucha infamia
y demasiado ejército,
y con esto no pueden los rugidos
de tus calderas, ni tus motores aéreos
ni tus grúas eléctricas y pavorosas
ni tus toneladas de desplazamiento.

¡Oh, portaviones *Intrépido*!,
tú en estas tórridas aguas de Santo Domingo
solamente por miedo.

Recoge, prodigioso milagro de la orilla,
tus dos anclas de hierro
y vete envuelto en pertinentes suavidades
y secretos,

vete al favor del diluido viento,
que hay pasiones y oscuros huracanes
en todo el archipiélago de las Antillas,
y no vuelvas, antes que el incendio
de todas las mujeres y los hombres
de todos los pueblos
alcancen lo que alcanzan en el mundo

ellos, solamente por cólera infinita

y tú,
        solamente por miedo.

1962

for many years have gone by, much blood
mixed with sweat and abuses,
much mutilation and much infamy
and too much army,
and this is too much for your roaring
boilers or your airplane motors
or your dreadful and electric cranes
or your tons of displacement.

Oh, carrier *Intrepid,*
you in these torrid waters of Santo Domingo
out of fear.

Raise, prodigious marvel of the shore,
your two iron anchors
and leave with your secrets wrapped
in an appropriate softness,

leave with the help of the diluted wind,
for there are passions and dark hurricanes
throughout the Antillean archipelago,
and do not come back, before the consuming passion
of all women and all men
of all peoples
achieves what is achieved throughout the world

by them, out of boundless rage

and you,
          out of fear.

1962

(DDW)

NI UN PASO ATRÁS

Árbol de luna que obedece al clima
en un sistema de nocturnidad,
no permitas que el muérdago te oprima.
Ni un paso atrás.

No permitas que el largo regimiento
de los años de crimen pertinaz,
te toque el hombro con el pensamiento.
Ni un paso atrás.

Que la alta flor que de tus ramas brota
en este chapuzón de libertad,
no pierda en miel ni la más breve gota.
Ni un paso atrás.

Ni un paso atrás, soldados y civiles
hermanados de pronto en la verdad.
La vida es una sobre los fusiles,
que no hay trincheras para los reptiles,
de malos nuestros a extranjeros viles.
Ni un paso atrás.

La libertad como un antiguo espejo
roto en la luz, se multiplica más,
y cada vez que un trozo da un reflejo
el tiempo nuevo le repite al viejo:
ni un paso atrás.

NOT ONE STEP BACK

Moonlit tree that responds to the climate
in a system of nocturnity,
do not let the mistletoe oppress you.
Not one step back.

Do not let the long regiment
of the years of relentless crime
touch your shoulder with the thought.
Not one step back.

May the lofty flower that sprouts from your branches
in this splash of freedom
not lose even the slightest drop of sweet nectar.
Not one step back.

Not one step back, soldiers and civilians
brothered suddenly in truth.
Life is made one above the guns,
for there are no trenches for snakes,
from our own wretches to vile foreigners.
Not one step back.

Freedom, like an old mirror
shattered in the light, is multiplied
and each time a fragment flashes back
the new time repeats to the old time:
not one step back.

Ni un paso atrás, ni un paso atrás, ni un paso
de retorno al ayer, ni la mitad
de un paso en el sentido del ocaso,
ni un paso atrás.

Que en la lucha del pueblo se confirme,
— sangre y sudor — la nacionalidad.
Y pecho al plomo y la conciencia en firme.
Y en cada corazón ni un paso atrás.

1965

Not one step back, not one step back, not one step
of return to yesterday, not half
a step in the direction of the setting sun,
not one step back.

Let nationhood — blood and sweat —
be proven in the people's fight.
Confronting bullets with a clear conscience.
And in each heart not one step back.

1965

(DDW)

AMÉN DE MARIPOSAS

El autor
y bajo el título de

Amén de mariposas

A LA EMBAJADORA NORTEAMERICANA
EN MÉXICO, EL AÑO DE 1914

porque, durante la ocupación de Veracruz por tropas
de su propio país, exclama:

"¡Ésta es la danza de la muerte
y creo que nosotros tocamos el violín!"

y por lo que en sus palabras suena de admonitorio,
de desgarrador y quién sabe si hasta de maternal,

dedica

este poema
cincuenta años después,
cuando es más alegre el gatillo del violín,
cuando más tumultuoso el delirio de la danza.

Mariposa:
caricatura de aeroplano.
Pulso de abismo,
erudita de pétalos.
Antes que las manos
en la pared to mataron
… los ojos de los niños …

PEDRO MA. CRUZ, *Raíces iluminadas*

AMEN TO BUTTERFLIES

The author
under the title of

Amen to Butterflies

TO THE WIFE OF THE AMERICAN AMBASSADOR
TO MEXICO, IN THE YEAR 1914

because, during the occupation of Vera Cruz by troops
from her own country, she exclaimed:

"This is the dance of death
and I think we are playing the violin!"

and because of what in his words sounds admonitory,
heartrending and maybe even maternal

dedicates

this poem
fifty years later,
when the trigger of the violin is merrier
when the delirium of the dance is more tumultuous.

Butterfly:
caricature of an airplane.
Pulse of the abyss,
scholar of petals.
Before the hands
killed you on the wall
… the eyes of the children …

PEDRO MA. CRUZ, *Raíces iluminadas*

PRIMER MOVEMENT

Cuando supe que habían caído las tres hermanas
     Mirabal
me dije:
     la sociedad establecida ha muerto.

     (Lapislázuli a cuento de todo emblema ruidoso
     mentís en A referido a un imperio en agonía
     y cuanto ha sido conocido desde entonces
                    me dije
     y cuanto ha sido comprendido desde entonces
                    me dije
     es que la sociedad establecida ha muerto)

Comprendí
que muchas unidades navales alrededor del mundo
              inician su naufragio
              en medio de la espuma
              pensadora
y que grandes ejércitos reconocidos en el planeta
              comienzan a derramarse
              en el regazo de la duda
              pesarosa
Es que
hay columnas de mármol impetuoso no rendidas al tiempo
y pirámides absolutos erigidas sobre las civilizaciones
que no pueden resistir la muerte de ciertas mariposas

FIRST MOVEMENT

When I learned that the three Mirabal sisters had
      fallen
I said to myself:
      established society is dead.

      (Lapis lazuli apropos of every noisy emblem
      denial in A referred to an empire in agony
      and all that has been known since then
                                 I said to myself
      and all that has been understood since then
                                   I said to myself
      is that established society is dead)

I understood
that many naval units around the world
                         initiate their shipwreck
                         amid the pensive
                         foam
and that great armies well known on the planet
                         begin to collapse
                         in the lap of grievous
                         doubt
It happens that
there are columns of impetuous marble not subdued by time
and perfect pyramids erected upon civilizations
that cannot endure the death of certain butterflies

Cuando supe que tres de los espejos de la sociedad
tres respetos del brazo y orgullo de los hombres
tres y entonces madres
                              y comienzo del día
              habían caído
              asesinadas
              oh asesinadas

       a pesar de sus telares en sonrisa
       a pesar de sus abriles en riachuelo
       a pesar de sus neblinas en reposo

(y todo el día lleno de grandes ojos abiertos)

              roto el cráneo
              despedazado el vientre
              partida la plegaria
              oh asesinadas

comprendí que el asesinato como bestia incendiada por la cola

              no se detendría ya

       ante ninguna puerta de concordia
       ante ninguna persiana de ternura
       ante ningún dintel ni balaustrada
                              ni ante paredes
                              ni ante rendijas

When I learned that three of society's mirrors
three refinements of the arm and the pride of men
three and at the time mothers
                                                and the day's beginning
                        had fallen
                        murdered
                        oh murdered

        despite their looms in the smile
        despite their Aprils in the brook
        despite their mists in repose

(and the whole day filled with big wide eyes)

                        the skull smashed
                        the womb ripped to pieces
                        the call to prayer scattered
                        oh murdered

I understood that murder like a beast with its tail in flames

                would not stop now

        at any door of concord
        at any shutter of tenderness
        at any threshold or balustrade
                                or at walls
                                or at crevices

ni ante el paroxismo
de los progenitores iniciales
porque a partir de entonces el plomo perdió su rumbo
y el sentido su rango
y sólo quedaba en pie
la Humanidad
emplazada a durar sobre este punto
escandaloso
de la inmensidad
del Universo
Supe entonces que el asesinato ocupaba el lugar
del pensamiento
que en la luz de la casa
comenzaba a aclimatarse
el puerco cimarrón
y la araña peluda
que la lechuza se instalaba en la escuela
que en los parques infantiles
se aposentaba el hurón
y el tiburón en las fuentes
y engranaje y puñal
y muñón y muleta
en los copos de la cuna
o que empezaba entonces la época rotunda
del bien y del mal
desnudos
frente a frente
conminados a una sola
implacable definitiva
decidida victoria
muerte a muerte

or at the paroxysm
of the first progenitors
because from then on bullets lost their direction
and meaning its rank
and left erect was only
Humanity
located to endure at this scandalous
point
in the immensity
of the Universe
I learned then that murder occupied the place
of thought
that by the light of the hearth
the wild boar
and the tarantula
were beginning to feel at home
that the owl was settling into the school
that in the playgrounds
the ferret was lodging
and the shark in the fountains
and gear and dagger
and stump and crutch
in the tufts of the cradle
or that then began the forthright Age
of good and evil
naked
face to face
instructed in one single
implacable definitive
determined victory
death to the death

Oh asesinadas
                    No era una vez
porque no puedo contar la historia de los hombres
                    que cayeron en Maimón
                    y Estero Hondo
                    a unos pocos disparos de Constanza
                    en el mismo corazón del año de 1959
puesto que todo el mundo sabe que somos el silencio
                    aun en horas de infortunio

No era una vez porque no puedo contar la historia
de este viejo país del que brotó la América Latina
puesto que todo el mundo sabe que brotó de sus vértebras
en una noche metálica denominada
                                        silencio

            de una vértebra llamada Esclavitud
            de otra vértebra llamada Encomienda
            de otra vértebra llamada Ingenio

y que de una gran vértebra dorsal le descendió
            completa
                    la Doctrina de Monroe

No contaré esta historia porque era una vez no la primera
que los hombres caían
            como caen los hombres
            con un gesto de fecundidad
para dotar de purísima sangre los músculos de la tierra

Oh murdered ones
                              it was not just once
for I cannot tell the story of the men
                  who fell at Maimón
                  and Estero Hondo
                  at a few shots from Constanza
                  in the very heart of 1959
since everyone knows that we are silence
                        even in times of misfortune

It was not just once for I cannot tell the story
of this old country from which sprang Latin America
since everyone knows that it sprang from her vertebrae
on a metallic night named
                  silence

      from a vertebra called Slavery
      from another vertebra called Royal Patronage
      from another vertebra called Plantation

and that from a great spinal column descended
      fully formed
            the Monroe Doctrine

I shall not tell this story because it was a time not the first
when men fell
      as men fall
      with an expression of fecundity
to endow with purest blood the muscles of the earth

La espada tiene una espiga
la espiga tiene una espera
la espera tiene una sangre
que invade a la verdadera

que invade al cañaveral
litoral y cordillera
y a todos se nos parece
de perfil en la bandera

la espiga tiene una espada
la espada una calavera

Pero un día se supo que tres veces el crepúsculo
tres veces el equilibrio de la maternidad
tres la continuación de nuestro territorio
sobre la superficie de los niños adyacentes
reconocidas las tres en la movida fiebre
                de los regazos y los biberones
protegidas las tres por la andadura
                de su maternidad navegadora
                navegable
                por el espejo de su matrimonio
                por la certeza de su vecindario
                por la armonia de su crecimiento
                y su triple escuela de amparo
habían caído en un mismo silencio asesinadas
                y eran las tres hermanas Mirabal
                oh asesinadas

The sword has a handle
the handle has a notch
the notch has a blood
that invades the true one

that invades the plantation
by the sea and in the mountains
and it appears to us all
in profile on the flag

the handle has a sword
the sword a skull

But one day it was learned that three times the twilight
three times the equilibrium of maternity
three the continuation of our territory
over the surface of the adjacent children
the three recognized in the frantic fever
     of laps and nursing bottles
the three protected by the pace
     of their navigating maternity
     navigable
     through the mirror of their marriage
     through the certainty of their neighbourhood
     through the harmony of their growth
     and their triple school of charity
had fallen in the same silence murdered
     that they were the three Mirabal sisters
       oh murdered

entonces se supo que ya no quedaba más
        que dentro de los cañones había pavor
        que la pólvora tenía miedo
        que el estampido sudaba espanto
        y el plomo lividez
y que entrábamos de lleno en la agonía de una edad
        que esto era el desenlace de la Era
                       Cristiana

Oh dormidas
oh delicadas
qué injuria de meditar

El mes de noviembre descendía sobre los hombros
como los árboles aún debajo de la noche y aún
                dando
                sombra
Oh eternas

El péndulo palpitaba las horas del municipio
y el pequeño reloj destilaba en silencio gota a gota
veinticinco visiones de un día llamado de noviembre

Pero aún no era el fin
oh dormidas
aún no era el fin
        no era el fin

then it was learned that there was nothing left
                    that inside the cannons there was terror
                    that the gunpowder was afraid
                    that the boom was sweating fright
                    and the lead lividity
that we were entering fully into the death throes of an Age
                    that this was the undoing of the Christian
                                        Era

Oh sleeping ones
oh delicate ones
what an injury to think on

The month of November descended upon the shoulders
like trees still under the night and still

                              giving
                              shade
Oh eternal ones

The pendulum pulses the hours of the municipality
and the little clock silently distilled drop by drop
twenty-five visions of a day said to be in November

But this was not yet the end
oh sleeping ones
it was not yet the end
                    it was not the end

SEGUNDO TIEMPO

Cuando supe que una pequeña inflamacíon del suelo
en el Cementerio de Arlington
se cubría de flores y manojos de lágrimas
con insistencia de pabellones y caballos nocturnos
alrededor de un toque de afligida trompeta
cuando todo periódico se abría en esas páginas
cuando se hicieron rojas todas las rosas amarillas
                    en Dallas
                    Texas
me dije
                    cómo era presidencial
                    el nuevo mes de noviembre

        ya millones de seres tocaron lo imposible
ya millones de seres ya millones de estatuas ya
        millones
                    de muros de columnas y de máquinas
                    comprendieron de súbito
                          que el asesinato
                                    no ha sido
        ni un fragmento de minuto

calculado solamente para las cabezas semicoloniales
                    y sustantivas
de las tres hermanas Mirabal

                    sino

SECOND MOVEMENT

When I learned that a small inflammation of the ground
in Arlington Cemetery
was covered with flowers and handfuls of tears
with an insistence on flags and horses at night
around the call of a grieving bugle
when every paper opened at those pages
when all the yellow roses turned red
                in Dallas
                Texas

I said to myself
                how presidential was
                the new month of November

        now millions of humans beings touched the impossible
now millions of human beings now millions of statues now
        millions
                of walls of columns and of machines
                        suddenly understood
                                that murder
                                        has not been
        not for a fragment of a minute

calculated only for the semicolonial and substantive heads
                of the three Mirabal sisters

                                but

que este inédito estilo de la muerte
producto de las manos de los hombres
        de manos del hermanos
            (por todo el siglo)
        muerte sana y artesana
            (por todo el mundo)
        provista de catálogo
            (por todo el tiempo)
de número de serie or serial number
y venida de fuera o made in usa

fría inalterable desdeñosa desde arriba desde
entonces
esta muerte
                    esta muerte
                                        esta muerte
asume contenido universal
forzosamente adscrita a la condición

            del ser humano
en cuyo espectro solar figuran todas las fórmulas
            personales

        y todas las instancias puras

            del individuo

                tal
        como va por la calle

that this unheard-of style of death
a product of the hands of men
  the hands of brothers
  (throughout the century)
  a sound and craftsmanlike death
  (throughout the world)
  provided with a catalogue
  (throughout all time)
with a series number or a serial number
and come from abroad or made in USA

cold unalterable disdainful from on high from
then on
this death
    this death
       this death
acquires a universal content
necessarily attributed to the condition

   of being human
in whose solar spectre appear all the personal
    formulas

  all the simple demands

   of the individual

    such
as going down the street

como habitante de la ciudad con todo su derecho como
continuador esencial del índice de población o séase
representante manufacturero indiferente agente de
seguros repartidor de leche asalariado guarda
campestre administrador o sabio o poeta o portador
de una botella de entusiasmo etílico donde están
convocadas todas las palabras

    ciclamen platabanda metempsícosis
    canícula claudia clavicémbalo
    cartulario venático vejiga
    trepa caterva mequetrefe
    primicia verdulero postulante
        palabras todas sustitutivas
        palabras pronunciables
        en lugar de presuntas actitudes
        y todas las maldiciones y protestas
        y las posiciones geométricas igual
        que la rotura del sentido igual
        que la rotura de una biela igual
        que el desgarrón de la barriga igual
        mente todo desquiciado y rom
        pido todo maligno y amargo
        todo reducido a sombra
            y nadidad y oscuridad
              y estadidad
        palabras mentirosas llenas
        de contenido impronunciable
        y desechos del organismo
        de cualquier muchacha iqual
        que de cualquier cochero igual

as a resident of the city with all his rights as
an essential propagator of the population index, that is
a manufacturer's representative an apathetic insurance agent
a salaried milkman a rural guard an administrator or
scholar or poet or bearer of a bottle of ethylic enthusiasm
where all words are convoked

      cyclamen flowerbed metempsychosis
      canicula claudia clavidcembalo
      chartulary mercurial vesicle
      scansorial multitude jackanapes
      first fruits green grocer postulant
          all substantive words
          pronounceable words
          in place of so-called attitudes
          and all the curses and protests
          and the geometrical positions just
          like the break in the sense just
          like the break in a tie rod just
          like the big rip in the belly just-
          ly all unhinged and bro-
          ken all maligned and bitter
          all reduced to shadow
               and nothingness and darkness
                  and beingness
        lying words full
        of unspeakable meaning
        and the remains of any
        girl's organ like
        that of any cabby just

que el choque tie la portezuela
del catafalco iqual

fue esta universal investidura de la que no está exento
nadie nadie
ni yo
ni tú
ni nosotros ni ellos ni nadie
podridamente nadie

nadie
desde el mismo momento en que fueron golpeadas
ciertamente
profesionalmente
maquinalmente

tres de las hermanas Mirabal

hasta llegar
en punto
exactamente
al
fin fin fin
de la Era
Cristiana

(Oigamos
oigamos
esto retumba en el
más
absoluto silencio

like the slamming of the door
of the catafalque just so

was this universal investiture from which is exempted
        nobody nobody
        neither I
        nor you
        nor we nor they nor nobody
        absolutely nobody

                nobody
from the very moment when they were struck down
        certainly
                professionally
                mechanically

    the three Mirabal sisters

                        until one arrives
                        on the dot
                        exactly
                        at the
                        end end end
                        of the Christian
                        Era

(Listen
listen
this reverberates in the
most
absolute silence

muchas unidades navales en todos los océanos inician
su hundimiento después
de deglutir los archipiélagos
de miel envenenada
grandes ejércitos destacados en la entrada del mundo
comienzan a reintegrarse
a sus viejos orígenes
de sudor y clamor
en el seno de las masas
populares

en el más
en el más categórico y el más
absoluto
silencio)

Porque

hay columnas de mármol impetuoso no rendidas al tiempo
y pirámides absolutas erigidas sobre las civilizaciones
que no pueden resistir la muerte de ciertas mariposas

y calles enteras de urbes imperiales llenas de transeúntes
sostenidas desde la base por tirantes y cuerdas de armonía
de padre a hija de joven a jovenzuela de escultor a modelo

y artilleros atormentados por la duda bajo el cráneo
cuyas miradas vuelan millares de leguas sobre el horizonte
para alcanzar un rostro flotante más allá de los mares

many naval units on all the oceans begin
                              their sinking after
                              devouring the archipelagos
                              of poisoned honey
great armies stationed at the entrance of the world
                              begin to return
                              to their old origins
                              of sweat and clamour
                              in the bosom of the masses
                              of the people

in the most
in the most categorical and the most
absolute
silence)

Because

there are columns of impetuous marble not subdued by time
and perfect pyramids erected upon civilizations
that cannot endure the death of certain butterflies

and entire streets of imperial cities filled with passersby
supported at the base by suspenders and harmonic chords
from father to daughter from boy to girl from sculptor to model

and gunners tormented by doubt beneath the skull
whose glances fly thousands of leagues over the horizon
to reach a countenance that floats beyond the seas

y camioneros rubios de grandes ojos azules obviamente veloces
que son los que dibujan o trazan las grandes carreteras
y transportan la grasa que engendra las bombas nucleares

y portaviones nuevos de planchas adineradas invencibles
insospechablemente unidos al rumbo de acero y del petróleo
y gigantes de miedo y fronteras de radar y divisiones aéreas
y artefactos electrónicos y máquinas infernales dirigidas
de la tierra hacia el mar y del cielo a la tierra y viceversa
que no pueden
       resistir
            la muerte
                 de ciertas
                      mariposas

porque la vida entera se sostiene sobre un eje de sangre
y hay pirámides muertas sobre el suelo que humillaron
porque el asesinato tiene que respetar si quiere ser respetado

y los grandes imperios deben medir sus pasos respetuosos
porque to necesariamente débil es lo necesariamente fuerte
cuando la sociedad establecida muere por los cuatro costados

cuando hay una hora en los relojes antiguos y los modernos
que anuncia que los más grandes imperios del planeta
no pueden resistir la muerte muerte

      de ciertas ciertas
            debilidades amén
                  de mariposas

and blond truckdrivers with big blue eyes obviously quick
who are the ones who draw or design great highways
and transport the slag that engenders nuclear bombs

and new aircraft carriers with invincible costly armour-plate
unexpectedly united in the course of steel and oil
and gigantic with fear and radar frontiers and aerial divisions
and electronic artifacts and infernal machines pointed
from land out to sea from heaven toward earth and viceversa
that cannot
                    endure
                            the death
                                    of certain
                                            butterflies

because life in its entirety is supported on an axis of blood
and there are pyramids dead upon the soil that they humiliated
because the murderer must show respect if he expects to be respected

and great empires must measure their respectful steps
because the necessarily weak is the necessarily strong
when established society is dying on all four flanks

when there is an hour on the ancient and modern clocks
announcing that the greatest empires on the planet
cannot endure the death death

        of certain certain
                    weaknesses amen
                            to butterflies

(DDW)

CONCIERTO DE ESPERANZA
PARA LA MANO IZQUIERDA

Amar y soportar; esperar pasta que la Esperanza cree
de sus propios despojos, aquello que anhela ...

— Shelley

INTRODUCCIÓN

Los rodillos cayeron sobre los guijarros. Y
la aurora al bailar devino polvareda.
¡Oh, todo quedó reducido a polvo! ¡Polvo!

Hasta las mismas lágrimas vertidas
recobran su estructura polvorienta.

Un justo anhelo de morir despierto
para no perdurar solamente dormido.

Una equidad o ecuación o igualdad
universal del asesinato. Y por lo mismo
todo en polvo y sinrazón como un antiguo piano.

A esto ha quedado reducido este país.

A polvo. Puesto que nada permanece en pie.
Ni en piedra ...

CONCERTO OF HOPE
FOR THE LEFT HAND

To love, and bear; to hope till Hope creates
From its own wreck the thing it contemplates ...

— Shelley

INTRODUCTION

The rollers fell on the cobblestones. And
dawn as she danced became a cloud of dust.
Oh, everything was left reduced to dust! Dust!

Even the very tears shed
reassume their dusty structure.

A just desire to die awake
so as not to merely survive asleep.

An equity or equation or universal
equality of murder. And for this reason
all to dust and injustice like an old piano.

This is what this country has been reduced to.

To dust. Since nothing is left erect.
Or in stone ...

Y continuando el argumento frío
con que está construido este concierto
no queda más que un pérfido compás
que repetidamente apaga al instrumento vida.

Dado que simplemente equilibrando el tiempo
sobre una tensa cuerda, la vibración ecuánime
comporta resultados que se extienden timbremente
por sin sobre tras de la contienda humana.

Y no admitamos que pudo sufrirse más y todavía
puede sufrirse más cuando es sabido
que una fuerza superior y más rentable
decide el contenido de nuestras existencias.

Se puede ser más débil que el final proyectado
se puede ser más débil todavía. Sin embargo
la naturaleza misma de los pueblos constituye
un sistema de violencia un coro de conmoción
que denodadamente restablece la asonancia vida.

Una violencia tal que como tal violencia
no es más que una respuesta sí o una respuesta no.

Y es así como ha sido decretado que la muerte
definitivamente debe morir, quedar cumplidamente
muerta, airadamente muerta la misma muerte.

And continuing the cold theme
on which this concerto is constructed
there remains only a perfidious rhythm
that repeatedly deadens the instrument's life.

Provided that by simply balancing the movement
upon a taut chord the even-tempered vibration
brings results that extend its timbre
throughout without over behind the human contest.

And let's not admit that more could be endured, and yet
more can be endured when it is known
that a superior and more profitable power
decides the content of our existence.

One can be weaker than the planned finale
one can be weaker still. And yet
the very nature of nations constitutes
a system of violence a choir of commotion
that boldly recasts harmony in life.

A violence such that as such violence
is no more than an answer yes or an answer no.

And so it has been decreed that death
must definitively die, must remain duly
dead, death itself violently dead.

Desplazada y borrada de las calles nocturnas
y los viejos caminos. Echada de las casas
universitarias y los sindicatos en huelga.
Proscrita de los ríos y las húmedas solitarias
celdas. Del Código Penal. Y de la isla
de Santo Domingo situada en el Mar Caribe
donde el asesinato por temor y por terror
anuncia su pertinez imperio sobre el mundo.

Displaced and erased from nocturnal streets
and the ancient roads. Cast out of college
dormitories and unions on strike.
Banished from rivers and damp solitary
cells. From the Penal Code. And from the island
of Santo Domingo situated in the Caribbean Sea
where murder through fear and through terror
announces its lasting dominion over the world.

A CAPRICCIO

Este concierto
no ha sido copiado
de manuscrito alguno.

No ha sido extraído
de ninguna botella
descubierta en la playa.

Ni en los bolsillos
de un centinela exacto
que se quedó dormido.

Ni en las bodegas
de un galeón hundido
desde entonces.

La herencia de algún
pirata no lo ha dejado
en la arena.

Ni siquiera ha sido
escuchado en un piano
de cola todavía.

Este concierto
obedece a su propia
concreta situación
porque en esencia
todo ha sido reducido
a polvo. ¡Polvo!

CAPRICCIO

This concerto
has not been copied
from any manuscript.

It has not been extracted
from any bottle
found on the beach.

Nor in the pockets
of a punctilious sentinel
who fell asleep.

Nor in the holds
of a galleon sunk
ever since then.

The legacy of some
pirate has not left it
on the sand.

It has not even
been heard on a grand
piano yet.

This concerto
responds to its own
concrete situation
because in essence
all has been reduced
to dust. Dust!

Y hay que ordenar
un toque de esperanza
al primer corneta
y al último redoblante
del batallón de
la mañana.

And we must order
a flourish of hope
from the first bugler
and from the last drummer
in the battalion of
the morning.

ANDANTE

Los rodillos cayeron sobre los guijarros
exactamente aquella mañana proyectada en almejas.

Mas no fue solamente sobre la isla de Santo
Domingo — denominada en el Mar Caribe
cálidamente
patria mía — sino mucho más lejos, traspasando
las anchas cordilleras y las zonas volcánicas
de todo planisferio. Fue una conducta planetaria.
Un ecuménico establecimiento del abuso.

Puesto que si el derecho de propiedad
está constituido por algunas palabras
que estabilizan a las corporaciones y sostienen
sobre la alta espuma a la marina mercante
es porque algunos hombres bajo algunos almendros
ejercen la razón de que su casa es suya.

Y continuando el argumento frío
que sirve de pentagrama a este concierto
la patria
es el derecho de propiedad más inviolable.

Y una patria es una sola patria
que cubre el universo en varios pasaportes
y no hay patria que se abalance sobre otra patria.

ANDANTE

The rollers fell upon the cobblestones
exactly that morning cast into shellfish.

But it was not only on this island of Santo
Domingo — warmly called in the Caribbean
Sea
my homeland — but much farther off, transcending
the sweeping cordilleras and the volcanic zones
of every planisphere. It was a planetary conduct.
An ecumenical establishment of betrayal.

Since if property rights
are constituted by a few words
that stabilize corporations and keep
the merchant marine on the high foam
it is because a few men under a few almond trees
reason that their home is their own.

And continuing the cold theme
that serves as stave to this concerto
the homeland
is the most inviolable of property rights.

And the homeland is a single homeland
that covers the universe in several passports
and there is no homeland that pounces on another homeland.

Y el tanque no es la norma física ni el portaviones
el orden natural. Ni el rascacielos constituye
por razones de acero un mandamiento irrevocable.
Ni la cibernética le ocurre al hombre
como una hemotisis. Puesto que entonces
la escala se desprende de las cuerdas
y asciende en espiral a las frecuencias
más vívidas, resuenan los trombones, la atmósfera
tiembla con la percusión desenfrenada del timbal
subdesarrollado, la orquesta universal retumba,
el gran concierto de la humanidad sacude
sus entrañas, el tímpano lanza un alarido,
las leyes históricas trepidan bajo las patas
de los contrabajos mientras los violoncelos
del corazón humano resuenan para estallar
estrepitosamente en todos los confines
en un desentumecido solo de esperanza.

And the tank is not the physical norm nor is the aircraft carrier
the natural order. Nor does the skyscraper constitute
for steely reasons an irrevocable commandment.
Nor do cybernetics occur to man
like a hemoptysis. Since at that time
the scale flies off the strings
and ascends in a spiral to the most vivid
frequencies, the trombones resound, the atmosphere
trembles with the unbridled percussion of the underdeveloped
kettledrum, the universal orchestra thunders,
the great concerto of humanity shakes
its insides, the timpani lets out a shriek,
the laws of history vibrate beneath the feet
of the double basses while the cellos
of the human heart resound and erupt
deafeningly throughout all the confines
in a rousing solo of hope.

SOLO DE ESPERANZA

La esperanza es un nido
y una semilla en el suelo.
La esperanza una flor
en forma de coliflor
que mastican lejanos
los camellos.
La esperanza es la raíz
en la humedad, y el arroyo
en el desierto.
El barco sobre la mar
y Federico en sus versos.
La esperanza es un concierto
popular
en los años duros
y en doscientos muertos.
El caballo en la montaña
y en Granada un monumento.
La esperanza es un cuartel
de policía consagrado
a cuidar la tranquilidad
del pensamiento
el orden del arcoíris
y la equidad del recuerdo.
La esperanza es la esperanza
convertida en ley
de los pueblos,
el pueblo convertido en ley
y la esperanza en Gobierno.

SOLO OF HOPE

Hope is a nest
and a seed in the ground.
Hope a flower
shaped like a cauliflower
chewed by far-off
camels.
Hope is the root
in the moisture, and the brook
in the desert.
The ship upon the sea
and Federico in his verses.
Hope is a people's
concerto
in hard years
and in two hundred dead.
The horse on the mountain
and in Granada a monument.
Hope is a police
barracks devoted
to looking after the peacefulness
of thought
the order of the rainbow
and the equity of remembrance.
Hope is hope
transformed into the law
of the peoples,
the people transformed into law
and hope into Government.

La esperanza es un Estado
de muchachas escribiendo
un plan quinquenal de niños
y una constitución del soneto.
La esperanza es contar con todo
lo que necesita el librero
y el obrero de obras públicas
para trazar un camino
que una a todos los pueblos
del mundo,
convierta a todas las patrias
en una sola patria,
reúna todos los brazos
en un solo trabajo
sideral y alegre,
lleve la flor y la coliflor
a los desiertos,
traiga invasiones de trigo
y de manzana a los centrales
azucareros.
Un río de lunas que gira
en el corazón del sistema
planetario y derrama
la médula del hombre
sobre la espuma del
firmamento.
La esperanza es la muerte
de lo que fuera antiguo
y ha sido eterno.
La esperanza es la muerte de la muerte.
La esperanza es la esperanza
de reanudar la juventud del pueblo.

Hope is a State
of girls writing
a five-year plan for children
and a constitution of the sonnet.
Hope is to count on everything
the needs of the bookseller
and the public-works worker
to lay out a road
that will unite all the peoples
of the world,
transform all the countries
into a single country,
link all the arms
in a single sidereal
and joyful effort,
carry the flower and the cauliflower
to the deserts,
bring invasions of wheat
and apple to the sugar
mills.
A river of moons spinning
in the heart of the planetary
system and spilling out
man's marrow
upon the foam of the
firmament.
Hope is the death
of what had been ancient
and has been eternal.
Hope is the death of death.
Hope is the hope
of renewing the people's youth.

GRAVE

¡Cuántos niños han muerto
a la sombra de nuestras esperanzas!
Nosotros los mayores no merecemos perdón.
Utilizamos la ternura para infundir
y las escuelas matutinas para inculcar
y las estatuas callejeras para inflijir
y los discursos en la plaza para perpetrar
y los manuales y las prédicas y los
premios dominicales y los programas
infantiles en la televisión y luego
los dejamos morir traspasados por
las bayonetas. ¡Cuántos niños han muerto
a la sombra de nuestras esperanzas!
Nosotros los mayores somos inventores
del cariño y luego productores de la bayoneta.
Nosotros acariciamos la esperanza y luego
somos los impávidos verdugos de la esperanza.
Hemos inventado la ley y el cumplimiento
de la ley. Hemos creado la vida y decretado
la muerte. Somos los treinta dineros
de nuestras propias alegrías. Merecemos
tristeza, merecemos eternamente la esperanza.
Vivir la realidad y estrangular
los sueños. Ajusticiarlos a quemarropa.
Ponerles nuestros nombres y asesinarlos.
Nosotros los mayores que hemos perdido
el respeto al pasado y asesinamos el futuro.
Los que decimos: ¡son los hijos ajenos!

GRAVE

How many children have died
in the shadow of our hopes!
We elders deserve no forgiveness.
We utilize tenderness to instill
and grade schools to inculcate
and statues in the streets to inflict
and speeches in the square to perpetuate
and manuals and sermons and
Sunday prizes and children's
programmes on television and then
we let them die pierced by
bayonets. How many children have died
in the shadow of our hopes!
We elders are inventors
of affection and then producers of the bayonet.
We nourish hope and then
we are the dauntless executioners of hope.
We have invented the law and compliance
with the law. We have created life and decreed
death. We are the thirty coins
of our own joys. We deserve
sadness, we deserve hope eternally.
Living reality and strangling
dreams. Executing them point-blank.
Giving them our names and murdering them.
We elders who have lost
respect for the past and who murder the future.
We who say: they are other people's children!

como si fueran ajenos nuestros hijos
como si fueran hijos del árbol o de las rocas
o del crepúsculo boreal como si fueran
hijos de la llama y del ornitorrinco
como si fueran hijos de otros sistemas
solaces o patrias cósmicas ultravioletas
como si nosotros los mayores no fuéramos
los padres de los hijos o si los hijos
de los mayores fueran los hijos de los menores.
Somos nosotros los culpables. Somos
los implacables destructores de nosotros mismos.
No merecemos perdón. Merecemos la esperanza
eternamente sumergidos en la esperanza.

as if our own children were the children of others
as if they were children of the tree or the rocks
or of the northern twilight as if they were
children of the flame and of the platypus
as if they were the children of other solar
systems or ultraviolet cosmic countries
as if we elders were not
the parents of the children or if the children
or the elders were the children of the young ones.
We are the guilty ones. We are
the implacable destroyers of ourselves.
We deserve no forgiveness. We deserve hope
eternally submerged in hope.

CADENCIA

La esperanza es un muerto
con los labios mordidos.

La esperanza es crispar
los puños frente al olvido.

La esperanza es un tema triste
que resuena en un río negro
que llevamos dentro.

La esperanza es un íntimo
rencor cuando los pueblos
se desangran, cuando ha visto
el mundo llenarse de clamor
y sacrificio
no solamente el alma
de Santo Domingo
sino el tiempo el corazón
unánime del siglo
en todos los idiomas
y todos los delirios.

La esperanza es la hora
de impulsar la marcha
del reloj, de practicar
el barco sobre la mar
y el caballo en la montaña
que amaba Federico.

CADENZA

Hope is a dead man
with bitten lips.

Hope is to clench
your fists facing oblivion.

Hope is a sad theme
echoing down a black river
that we bear within us.

Hope is a private
bitterness when a people
bleeds to death, when the world
has seen itself filled with clamour
and sacrifice
not only the soul
of Santo Domingo
but the movement the unanimous
heart of the century
in all languages
and all ravings.

Hope is the hour
of winding
the clock, of piloting
the ship upon the sea
and the horse on the mountain
that Federico loved.

La esperanza es el fin
de la Humanidad
si no torcemos el rumbo
del rodillo
si una antorcha y un puño
no alzan los volcanes
y desbordan los ríos
de redención en redención
hasta la carcajada de los niños.

La esperanza es la última
vez
cuando por delante y por detrás
no queda otro camino
que la realidad golpeante
y golpeable
palpitante y palpitable
como un vals
sobre los cinco sentidos.

La esperanza es el fin
de la esperanza
y el comienzo
del destino
de la esperanza.

Hope is the end
of Humanity
if we do not shift the course
of the steamroller
if the volcanoes do not raise
a torch and a fist
and rivers overflow
from redemption to redemption
till reaching the wild laughter of the children.

Hope is the last
time
when in front and in back
there is no other way
except reality pounding
and poundable
throbbing and throbbable
like a waltz
on the five senses.

Hope is hope's
end
and the beginning
of hope's
destiny.

DIANA

Este concierto
ha sido escrito
para una sola mano
porque en esencia
todo ha sido reducido
a polvo. ¡Polvo!
Y no subsiste nada.
Ni en pie ni en piedra.

Apenas la esperanza
llenándose de muerte
y esperando la muerte
de la esperanza
la abolible agonía
de la esperanza
cuando ya reverbera
la radiante explosión
de la realidad
brotando de los despojos
de la esperanza.

Y aquí concluye
entre nosotros
este convicto concierto
de la esperanza.

REVEILLE

This concerto
has been written
for a single hand
because in essence
all has been reduced
to dust. Dust!
And nothing endures.
Either erect or in stone.

Hope scarcely
filling itself with death
and hoping for the death
of hope
the revocable agony
of hope
when the radiant explosion
of reality
now shimmers
flaring forth from the rubble
of hope.

And here ends
among us
this condemned concerto
of hope.

(DDW)

MEDITACIÓN A ORILLAS DE LA TARDE

Plurales, los pueblos del Caribe, silenciosos
algunos, otros tristes y anónimos, y algunos
salidos de la fuente del olvido, como ocurre
    cada vez que la noche se detiene en un recodo
    junto a una ventana persuasiva,
                  duermen.

Duermen. Tal vez inolvidablemente, con palabras
dulces sobre un incomprendido mármol. "Aquí complace
su inquietud eterna un alma innumerable." Y es un pueblo
cualquiera del Caribe. No, no es un pueblo cualquiera.
Es la orilla alucinante en que un talón resbala
o lucha. Pendiente clave junto a una herida nota.

Nota salvaje de tambor o cuero.

Atento a todo, un poderoso empuje de molino.
Situado en estas vísperas mortales, sin quererlo
llama a todos a enarbolar la lanza
y el jamelgo y el burro necesariamente
porque somos nudos de un mismo tallo
y nuestras hambres y nuestros sueños
se reconocen por los mismos gestos y las mismas
obras. Debemos comprendernos con soltura
frente al molino. Flacos, poseídos, pobres
y gesticulantes, sin saber de qué agria disciplina
nos procede esta marca y esta lucha, pero juntos.
Siempre juntos frente at molino.

MEDITATION ON THE SHORES OF EVENING

So many, the peoples of the Caribbean, silent
some of them, others sad and nameless, and some
risen from the fountain of oblivion, as happens
      every time night pauses at a bend in the road
      before a beckoning window,
                           they are asleep.

They are asleep. Perhaps unforgettably, with tender
words upon an unsung marble stone. "Here satisfies
her eternal restlessness a countless soul." And it is any
one of the Caribbean peoples. No, not just any one.
It is the illusory shore on which a heel slips
or struggles. A key dangling beside a wounded note.

A savage note of drum or leather.

Watchful of everything, a powerful windmill thrust.
Situated upon these mortal verges, unwillingly
he calls on everyone to raise the lance,
and the nag and the burro must rear up
because we are all knots of a single stem
and our hungers and our dreams
sense each other through the same gestures and same
works. We must understand each other implicitly
facing the windmill. Emaciated, crazed, penniless
and grimacing, not knowing from what harsh discipline
this mark and this struggle befall us, but bound as one.
Always bound as one facing the windmill.

Siempre el molino y esta vez con aspas
silenciosas e insinuantes, su vientre financiero,
su flor registradora, intransferible, su tibia
sucursal en todo el mundo como un cuarto menguante.

Pero aquí estamos todos con la misma
rodilla clavada en nuestras tierras. Oro antiguo
que nos corre desde entonces, desde aquellas
floridas carabelas en forma de gaviotas,
por estas mismas venal enlazadas en hábitos,
heridas y colores, recibido en el beso
de nuestras rodillas simples y seculares,
en el arco brusco del lomo; el oro, el oro antiguo
avejenta el molino, lo sofoca, lo revienta,
y por nosotros se encabrita el potro,
y un burro joven huele los refranes, juega a Sancho,
cuando una lanza erguida suena en la pared del aire.

Seremos felices, nosotros los pueblos del Caribe.
Nuestras familes lianas regresarán del sueño.
Vamos a usar los nombres recogidos, de pronto,
como una brizna flotante que rueda con la espuma
al exprimir el viaje. Seremos felices, ya no cabe
duda. No cabe duda. Hay que limpiar la casa.
En todas partes ruge cierto animal de limpieza.

Es justo que nos regocijemos y que nos decidamos.
Triunfa nuestro apellido emancipado y mestizo.
¡Claro! Hemos sufrido mucho y nuestra sangre
ha enriquecido a muchos, ¡ya era hora! Saludemos
la hora. Ciertamente, saludemos la hora y el día,
y venga también el mes y todo el calendario.

Always the windmill and this time with its silent
insinuating crossed arms, its banker's belly,
its registrar's flower, nontransferable, its cool
branch offices the world over like a waning moon.

But here we all are with the same
knees driven into our lands. Ancient gold
that has cursed us ever since, ever since
those flowering caravels shaped like seagulls,
has run through these same veins joined by habits,
wounds and colours, gold received in the kiss
of our poor and century-old knees,
in the abrupt arch of our backs; gold, ancient gold
ages the windmill, suffocates it, works it to death,
and because of us the colt rears up
and a young burro sniffs at sayings, plays Sancho,
when a raised lance rings against the wall of air.

We shall be happy, we peoples of the Caribbean.
Our simple families will return from the dream.
We shall bear all the names gathered up, suddenly,
like a floating wisp rolling in with the foam
at the journey's end. We shall be happy, there is
no doubt. None whatsoever. We must clean our house.
Everywhere a certain beast of cleanliness is roaring.

It is right and just that we rejoice and decide.
Our emancipated, mestizo name is victorious.
Yes, of course! We have suffered much and our blood
has enriched many. It was time! Let us greet
the hour. Yes, let us greet the hour and the day,
and let the month and the whole calendar come, too.

Este momento gusta y solicita. Nuestro es.
De ahora en adelante cambiaremos la sangre
de negocio en sangre de martirio o for de triunfo.

Ésta es aquella meditación tranquila que digo a ustedes
sosegadamente y a orillas de la tarde.
frente por frente del inmenso regazo tórrido del mar
      Caribe.

This moment pleases and attracts. It is our moment.
From this moment on we shall transform the blood of
business into the blood of martyrdom or victory's flower.

So this is that tranquil meditation that I'm telling you
at peace and on the shores of evening
face to face with the immense torrid lap of the Caribbean
        Sea.

(DDW)

SELECTED BIBLIOGRAPHY

Works by Pedro Mir

Poetry

Hay un país en el mundo. Havana: Talleres de La Campaña Cubana, 1949. Other eds., Santo Domingo: Ediciones Claridad, 1962; Santo Domingo: Editora Taller, 1976.

Contracanto a Walt Whitman; canto a nosotros mismos. Guatemala: Ediciones Saker-Ti, 1952.

Amén de mariposas. Santo Domingo: Nuevo Mundo, 1969.

Poemas de buen amor y a veces de fantasía. Santo Domingo: Nuevo Mundo, 1969.

El huracán Neruda: elegía con una canción desesperada. Santo Domingo: Taller, 1974.

Primeros poemas (1937-1947). In preparation.

Compilations and Anthologies

Viaje a la muchedumbre. [Anthology] Santo Domingo: Ediciones Lucerna, 1971. Other ed., with a prologue by Jaime Labastida, Mexico: Siglo XXI, 1972.

Poemas de una isla y de dos pueblos. Havana: Casa de las Américas, 1974.

Hay un país en el mundo y otros poemas. Santo Domingo: Taller, 1982. [Contains almost all of Mir's poetic works.]

Homenaje a Pedro Mir. [Anthology] Santo Domingo: Editora Alfa & Omega, 1983.

Fiction

La gran hazaña de limber y después otoño. Santo Domingo: Sargazo, 1977.

Cuando amaban las tierras comuneras. Mexico: Siglo XXI, 1978.

Buen viaje, Rancho Valentín! (memorias de un marinero). Santo Domingo: Taller, 1981.

Other Writings

El color del camino, photographs by Domingo Batista with an introduction and text by Pedro Mir, Santo Domingo, 1981.

Essays

Tres leyendas de colores: ensayo de interpretación de las tres primeras revoluciones del Nuevo Mundo. Santo Domingo: Editora Nacional, 1969.

Apertura a la estética. Santo Domingo: Universidad Autónoma de Santo Domingo, 1974.

Las dos patrias de Santo Domingo. Santo Domingo: Editora Cultural Dominicana, 1975.

El gran incendio: los balbuceos americanos del capitalismo mundial. 3rd. ed., Santo Domingo: Ediciones del Taller, 1978.

Fundamentos de teoría y crítica de arte. Santo Domingo: Universidad Autónoma de Santo Domingo, 1979.

La noción de periodo en la historia dominicana. Santo Domingo: Universidad Autónoma de Santo Domingo, 1981.

Las raíces dominicanas de la Doctrina de Monroe. Santo Domingo: Taller, 1984.

Historia del hambre en la República Dominicana. Santo Domingo: Editora Corripio, 1987.

La estética del soldadito. Santo Domingo: Editora Universidad-UASD, 1991.

El lapicida de los ojos morados (una semiótica de la poesía). In preparation.

Works in English Translation

"Amen to Butterflies". Trans. Roberto Márquez. *Latin American Revolutionary Poetry.* New York: Monthly Review Press, 1974. 210-31.

"Countersong to Walt Whitman" [Sections 1,6,9,15,17]. Trans. Didier Tisdel Jaén. *Homage to Walt Whitman.* Tuscaloosa: University of Alabama Press, 1969. 30-41.

"Countersong to Walt Whitman" [Preface & Sections 1-6]. Trans. Donald D. Walsh. *Review* 17 (1976): 35-38.
"Elegy for the 14th of June." Trans. Donald D. Walsh. *Street Magazine* 2.3 (1977): 22-23.
"Exile's Ballad, The". Trans. Donald D. Walsh. *Street Magazine* 2.3 (1977): 23-24.

Works About Pedro Mir

Alcántara Almanzar, José. "Pedro Mir," in *Estudios de poesía dominicana* (Santo Domingo, Dominican Republic: Edit. Alfa y Omega, 1979), pp. 219-242.

Arvelo, Alejandro. "Marxismo versus racionalismo en el capítulo sobre hegal del libro *Apertura a la estética de Pedro Mir.*" *Cuadernos de Poética* 1:2 (1984), 53-59.

Azurdui, Victoria. "Pedro Mir, voz grande de la poesía latinoamericana," Periódico *El Día,* Mexico, May 8, 1975.

Catalá, Rafael. "Una lectura de 'Autorretrato' de Pedro Mir." *Caribe* 12 (University of Hawaii, Honolulu, Hawaii, 1976), 95-108.

———. "Evolución del pensamiento en poetas del Caribe: Manuel Navarro Luna, Clemente Soto Vélez y Pedro Mir". *Alcance* 1:2 (1983), 18-22. Reproduced in Rose S. Minc (ed.), *Literatures in Transition: The Many Voices of the Caribbean Area: A Symposium* (Upper Montclair, NJ: Hispamérica, Montclair State College, 1982, pp. 97-106.

Fernández-Fragoso, Víctor. "De la noche a la muchedumbre: los cantos épicos de Pedro Mir." Doctoral dissertation. University of Connecticut, 1978.

García Lorenzo, Orlando. "Historia y poesía en Pedro Mir". *Bohemia* 76:5 (1984), 16-19.

Gonzalez, Otto-Raúl. "Con Pedro Mir en Isla de Pinos". *Revista Mexicana de Cultura,* February 1976.

Gutiérrez, Franklin. "Estructura poética en la obra de Pedro Mir". *Alcance: Revista Literaria 1:1* (1983), 3-4.

Hernández Rueda, Lupo. "Pedro Mir", in *La generación del 48 en la literatura dominicana* (Santiago, Dominican Republic: Universidad

Católica Madre y Maestra, 1981), pp. 130-134.

Inchaústegui Cabral, Héctor. "Pedro Mir", in *Escritores y artistas dominicanos* (Santiago, Dominican Republic: Universidad Católica Madre y Maestra, 1978), pp. 173-174.

Labastida, Jaime. "El viaje de Pedro Mir hacia la muchedumbre", prologue to *Viaje a la muchedumbre* by Pedro Mir (Mexico: Siglo XXI, 1972), pp. IX-XIV.

Maldonado Denis, Manuel. *"Viaje a la muchedumbre". Claridad* (8 July 1973), 22.

———. *"Pedro Mir, poeta antillano". Claridad,* San Juan de Puerto Rico, (8 April 1973).

Martínez-Clark, Ruth. "There Is a Country in the World and Other Poems of Pedro Mir", Bennington, Vermont. Bachelor of Arts thesis, Bennington College, 1988.

Matos Moquete, Manuel. "Poética política en la poesía de Pedro Mir". *Cuadernos de Poética* 5:13 (1987), 5-21. Also in *Revista Iberoamericana* 142 (1988), 199-211.

Pérez-Montaner, Jaime. "Walt Whitman en mangas de camisa". *Chasqui* 3:3 (1974), 50-55.

Pieter, Leo. "La realización del ser humano en el contracanto a Walt Whitman, Pedro Mir". (Santo Domingo, Dominican Republic, USAD, 1980), Editora Casanova. Doctoral dissertation.

Piña Contreras, Guillermo. "Pedro Mir". [Interview] in *Doce en la literatura dominicana* (Santiago, Dominican Republic: Universidad Católica Madre y Maestra, 1982), pp. 91-111.

Rivera Martínez, Mildred. "Juan Bosch y Pedro Mir: dos diálogos sobre la sociedad y la cultura dominicana (1885-1915)". *Nuevo Texto Crítico* 1:1 (1988), 151-174.

Rosario Candelier, Bruno. *"Hay un país en el mundo* (Evocación de Pedro Mir)". *Eme Eme: Estudios Dominicanos* 8:47 (1980), 37-40. Reproduced in Bruno Rosario Candelier (ed.), *Ensayos criticos: análisis de textos dominicanos contemporáneos* (Santiago, Dominican Republic: Universidad Católica Madre y Maestra, 1982), pp. 159-163.

Santana, Joaquín. "Pedro Mir: ¡Mi poesía es hija del exilio!" [Interview] OCLAE 4 (1978), 13.

Santiago Pedrosa, José. "Viaje a la muchedumbre de Pedro Mir. Hay un país en el mundo. Rio Piedras, Puerto Rico: Universidad de Puerto Rico, 1979. Doctoral dissertation.

Santos Moray, Mercedes. "Mir en primera plana". *Casa de las Américas* 15:90 (1975), 138-141.

———. "Tres poetas de una isla". *Casa de las Américas* 15:90 (1975), 138-141.

Schmidt-Rodríguez, Aileen. "Tras el secreto de la creación literaria: entrevista a Pedro Mir". *Arieto* 10:38 (1984), 39-40.

Torres-Saillant, Silvio. "Caribbean Poetics: Aesthetics of Marginality in West Indian Literature". [Pedro Mir, Edward Kamau Brathwaite, René Depestre]. Doctoral dissertation. New York University, 1991.

ALSO FROM PEEPAL TREE

Nicolás Guillén
Yoruba from Cuba: Selected Poems
Translated by Salvador Ortiz-Carboneres
ISBN: 9781900715973; pp. 180; pub. 2005; price £9.99

In calling this collection *Yoruba from Cuba*, a phrase from the poem 'Son Número 6', the translator, Salvador Ortiz-Carboneres, draws attention to Guillén's pioneering embrace, more than seventy years ago, of an African identity in Cuba. His selection shows Guillén constantly returning to the theme of race and the historical legacies of slavery in both the Caribbean and the USA. But in poems such as 'Balada de los Dos Abuelos', Guillén is also seen stressing the *mulatez* heterogeneity of Cuban culture in drawing on African, European and other immigrant traditions.

As a life-long Marxist and anti-imperialist, Guillén celebrated the Cuban revolution, including the heroic example of Che Guevara, but he also addressed the tendency to a repressive puritanism within the ruling party in such important poems as 'Digo que yo no soy un hombre puro'.

In this dual language selection of one of the outstanding poets of the Hispanic world, Salvador Ortiz-Carboneres has created lively, very readable English versions that capture both the colloquial vigour of Guillén's language and the incantatory rhythms of those of the poems where he draws on the dance patterns of the Cuban 'son'.

The selection covers the range of Guillén's work from *Poemas de Transición* (1927-1931) up to poems from *La Rueda Dentada* and *El Diario que a Diario*, both of 1972. With a translator's preface, an introduction by the distinguished scholar of Cuban culture, Professor Alistair Hennessy, notes, a chronology and a reading list, this is an edition that will bring Guillén's powerful and epochal poetry to both the general reader and to the student.

His work is unquestionably one of the towering landmarks of Caribbean poetry.